# My Morning Musings

## A Collection of Thoughts to Encourage Your Daily Walk

J. Katrinda McQueen

Cocoon to Wings
PUBLISHING

# MY MORNING MUSINGS

Printed in the United States of America

ISBN: 978-1-953497-66-6 (Paperback)

ISBN: 978-1-953497-68-0 (Digital)

Library of Congress Control Number: 2023913858

Published by Cocoon to Wings Publishing

7810 Gall Blvd., #311

Zephyrhills, FL 33541

www.CocoontoWingsBooks.com

(813) 906-WING (9464)

Book cover design by Kenya (Robinson)

# My Morning Musings

## A Collection of Thoughts to Encourage Your Daily Walk

Cocoon to Wings
PUBLISHING

# Dedication

To the people who are the reason I am,
Neal and Doris McQueen.

# *Acknowledgements*

---

In the tradition of the African American Church, first giving honor to God who is the head of my life. I give honor to Him in whom I live, I breathe, and I have my being. Thank you for gifting me with the ability to put pen to paper. Thank you for being my spirit guide.

There are so many people to thank, for so many reasons. Thank you to every person who has ever read anything that I have written. To those who read my writings, especially in the early days, I thank you for the encouragement and the confidence you had in my abilities, even before I had confidence in myself. Every time one of you suggested I put these messages in a book, you instilled a faith and belief in me that I will be eternally grateful for.

I will not name names… lest I forget someone. It sounds a bit cliché – but you know who you are. My family: birth, immediate, and extended. My littles. My gang, my guys, my fellas, my dudes. My sisters, my posse, my sistahs, my girls – Thank you.

I love you Moses.

# Table of Musings

# Introduction

As the English language continues to evolve, many words that were once part of daily conversation have faded away. Think about "thee" and "thou." Anyone using those words today is looked at with a cautious glance and people likely start to move away. If words manage to survive sociological evolution, their meanings often either change completely or expand to take on new definitions and context.

**Muse:**

A simple Google search of "muse" offers two definitions of the word as a noun. First, "(in Greek and Roman mythology) [it refers to] each of nine goddesses, the daughters of Zeus and Mnemosyne, who preside over the arts and sciences and then as "a person or personified force who is the source of inspiration for a creative artist. "Yeats' muse, Maud Gonne." For those of us that grew up on Webster's Dictionary, now referred to as Merriam-Webster, an additional context is offered for the word as a verb: "to become absorbed in thought especially to think about something carefully and thoroughly musing about what might have been."[1] Merriam-Webster also offers us a definition of the word as a noun: "a source of inspiration *especially* a guiding genius." Hence: My Morning Musings.

The words on the pages that follow have been a source of inspiration to me. Presented as hard, cold, facts – these words have sustained me and kept me. As we say in the Southern Baptist Church, these words have "kept me from dangers seen and unseen." That phrase is generally used in context with the keeping power of our Lord and Savior Jesus Christ, and that context is appropriate here. While I may have been the one to put the words on paper, there is absolutely no doubt that these words were inspired, directed, and guided by God. My guiding genius. My muse.

Why me? When spoken, these two words can be an exclamation of hope or despair. More often than not, they are the words we utter when we are trying to understand something that has taken place in our lives... something we have not planned for, expected, or desired.

In the life of the believer, this question is often posed softly. Many of us were taught that asking questions of God was just short of asking for an invitation to be sent straight to the pits of hell. How dare we imply that God does not know what is going on with us, or worse still, that He does not know what He is doing! Despite these perceived implications, we are human beings made by a God who is all-knowing and all-seeing... and yes, even all-hearing, and that means He hears us when we ask, "Why Me?"

In April 2018, I found myself in a new city -- my new home after more than three decades in the same city. I experienced a complete range of emotions from excitement to pure trepidation as I worked to try to expand the high of the excitement and to extinguish the anxiety that came with the trepidation. Lest anyone think that this new city was a stop along the way to my place of banishment for questioning God, I must admit, I was in the city by choice… or so I thought.

The situations that led to this choice are wrapped up in the death of a loved one, the loss of a job, a change in social status (or so I thought), and emotional and physical unrest – all things that I thought a fresh start would resolve.

The new city offered its own set of challenges beginning with the fact that I knew absolutely no one other than a few of the people I would be working with. The weight of the changes manifested on day one… being alone in a new city (not counting my fur baby, Bella), a new job, a new address, no church, no family, no friends -- none of the important stuff-- no hair stylist, no nail technician, no doctor, not knowing how to navigate; coping became a full-time job that started every day long before my paying job. It also came with a 24/7 schedule.

I have long wanted to be a morning person. Perhaps after watching too much television, I have wanted to be that person that wakes up every morning refreshed – excited about getting up and starting the day. I admire the person who spends quiet time with God and is grateful, thankful, and reflective. Despite my six decades plus of life, I am not that person. Never have been… and I am not sure I ever will be. That does not stop me from trying. To help me cope, I took on the task of getting up and spending time each morning, mainly asking God how I came to be in this place -- a place that felt really, really good at times and a place that felt really desolate at times. Really, really desolate.

Every day, I woke up thankful that God gave me another day. Thankful, grateful, and scared. Scared of what the day was going to offer and even more afraid of whether I could handle whatever was ahead. So, I spent my mornings in conversation with God, asking, and more often than not - pleading, for Him to show me what to do, how to do it, and when to do it.

My Morning Musings. My guiding genius. Many times, the words would come faster than I could comprehend and certainly faster than I could write. At times, I could not understand the message or what I was supposed to do with what I was being given. So, since I do words for a living, I started to write. Often when I started to write, I would wonder what the meaning of the message was since it did not seem to apply to me. I asked what I was supposed to do with these messages (musings), and He said to share. And I did. I shared these as my daily posts on Facebook. Many of you commented. Many of the comments encouraged me to put the posts in a book, and that is what I did. Here are my morning musings.

# Opening Doors

"God loves you too much to open the wrong doors. He is not letting you down, He's doing you a favor."

I am not sure who said this or why, but it is hard for me to believe right now. When someone typically asks, "Will you do me a favor?" they usually are asking if you will do something to help, something to lift them up and not to hurt them. If this is the right door for me right now, it sure does not feel like it.

But isn't that what knowing God is really all about? Not what you feel, but what you know?

There are so many scriptures that tell us that we should walk by faith and not by sight (2 Corinthians 5:7) and that His ways are not our ways (Isaiah 55:8-9). You have to look a little harder to find the scriptures that tell you how to do this, but they are there.

It is His love. He loves you. Period. Full stop. No matter what it feels like, God loves you. He loves you more than you could ever imagine or even know. He loves even in those times when you feel unlovable. In the process of working to understand God's love, couple it with the acceptance that He is in the right-door, lift-you-up business. No matter what it feels like, the knowing is what will get you through.

God, will you do me a favor? He said, Yes!

# Plowing Lessons

"You simply have to put one foot in front of the other and keep going. Put blinders on and plow right ahead." ~ George Lucas, American filmmaker

Most of us don't know firsthand what plowing is actually like. The goal of plowing is to keep moving at a pace that allows for a row that is wide enough, deep enough, and long enough to plant seeds to yield a good harvest. If you break your pace, even for a brief rest, you run the risk of the row shifting when you start back up.

Getting through the grind of everyday life is a bit like plowing. Put one foot in front of the other and keep going. Even when you keep going, you have to stay focused – keeping your eyes peering straight ahead – on the task ahead – to the end of the row. The only way to get this done is to keep moving. Thanks, George Lucas, for an awesome quote.

# Learning How to Fall

"Sometimes you fall down, because there is something down there that you are supposed to find." ~ Dr. Travis Bradberry, author

In all of the various curriculums and courses that most students are part of in our twelve years of schooling, I do not recall a single one that teaches us how to fall. So, where and when do we learn how to fall down and what to do when we fall?

If you have ever observed a toddler who is learning to walk, their focus is on standing up and moving forward. As the parent or adult in the room, our focus is on hoping they will not fall. This is a futile hope because falling is part of the learning process. They are surely going to fall. The toddler is excited about the coaching and encouragement they are given as they make repeated efforts to stand, let go, and move forward. It fuels their desire to keep trying. But how do we respond when they fall?

Too often, we rush to console in what may not even be a consolable moment. They fell, bottom first on the carpeted floor. What is there to console? Why should they be sad? When this happens and our rapid response is to rush to them, we inadvertently teach them that falling down is bad. Falling down is not bad; it is falling down and hitting your head on the concrete that is bad.

We are even worse as adults. When we fall on the carpeted floor, it is not bad. When we fall on the concrete and hit our heads – it can be uncomfortable and slow us down for a bit. Concussion protocol says you have to sit out a few plays. I think this is what Dr. Bradberry is telling us. When you fall, do not be in such a hurry to get up. Take time, check yourself for bruises and then pause. Sometimes when you fall, it is for you to look around and see what you are supposed to be learning in that instance. What is down there that you need to find?

# My Intercessory Prayer For You

God bless you.
God bless your heart.
God bless your life.
God bless your health.
God bless your home.
God bless your family.
God bless your work.
God bless your spiritual life.
God bless your finances.
God bless all your projects.
God bless you and your family abundantly.

Choose who you want to pray over for God to bless today.

# Songs

Songs are words of encouragement that have the added gift of a melody. Woke up with this one on my heart and I am using it to encourage the start of the day.

"My faith looks up to Thee, Thou Lamb of Calvary,
Savior Divine; Now hear me while I pray;
Take all my guilt away; Oh, let me from this day
Be wholly Thine.

May Thy rich grace impart; Strength to my fainting heart,
My zeal inspire; As Thou hast died for me,
Oh, may my love to Thee, Pure, warm, and changeless be,
A living fire." ~ My Faith Looks Up to Thee by Ray Palmer
(Public Domain, 1830)

# Fasting

I am still amazed by the 21-day fast. Fasting is about letting go, sacrificing, and giving up. That is usually where most of us stop. The part we miss is that the intent of giving up something, abstaining from something - is to make room for God. It is to be able to spend more time with Him, seeking Him (and you will need to seek Him to get past the first seven-to ten days! I called it Hell Week!).

Keep in mind that you are seeking Him to receive strength, and to become mentally strong – strong enough to let go of things that don't serve us well and more importantly, strong enough to let go of things that do not equip us to do better, be better, have better... or equip us to walk fully in the life He has called us to. Footnote: we have to also be strong enough to remember not to go back to things that God has freed us from.

# New Car Smell

The word "new" makes us think of fresh and shiny, something that has not been tainted by the treatment of others. One of the most common experiences of something new is a "new car". That "new car smell," is distinct. It sends the message that the environment is "new" and has not been polluted by the smells and odors that represent life. The new car smell means things that have not been used.

Entering a new year does not mean new, shiny things... it means a new chance for our old things, and our old selves. Today, I am grateful for the old – and the old me that has been gifted with another chance.

# Still Here

After a few days of silence – a few exceedingly difficult days – God reminded me this morning, *I am still here. In fact, when you do not see me or feel me, that is when I am most there.* "Lo, I am with you always!" Matthew 28:20

(IMAGE CREDIT: J. KATRINDA McQUEEN JANUARY 9, 2020)

# A - New

I do words for a living. Words matter. Spaces matter also, as in "a new" versus "anew." This is the start of "a new" week. "New" is an adjective that means not existing before or for the first time. (Yahoo.com)[2] There are no conditions or descriptors associated when it appears like this.

"Anew" is an adverb. It means in a new or different and typically more positive way. (Yahoo.com)[3] Key words: different, more positive.

My week has begun "anew." It is different and more positive. **Different**: not the same as last week. **Positive**: I woke up to see another day, another week, the sixth day of the month, the 4th month of the year. **Positive**: I have shelter, food, clothing, sight, and the ability to write this message. I am even "clothed in my right mind."

Let our day begin anew, our week begin anew, and most of all, our hearts and spirits be "renewed."

# Planning In Pencil

I am a planner at heart. I function best when I have planned my day, my week, my month, the next 100 days, the next 6 months... the rest of the year. I even have a 2-5-7-10 plan (2-year, 5-year, 7-year, 10-year plan). I have tried probably every planner system made (and can give you honest feedback on ALL of them), and I have even tried my own planning system. And for these planning tools, you must have just the right pen. It has to feel good in your hands and write really well, or so I thought. The right system is still a work in progress.

I am a planner at heart. So much so, that one of my businesses is named P1634... representative of Proverbs 16:3-4. In the New International Version (NIV) it reads, "Commit to the Lord whatever you do, and he will establish your plans. The Lord works out everything to its proper end—even the wicked for a day of disaster."

In the process of perfecting my planning skills, I learned that even the best laid plan is destined to fail if we do not seek Him and His will [for our plans]. Even though He is gracious and allows us to make plans and to chart out what WE think we want and need, what WE think is best for us... those plans still have to be committed to Him. We must pledge our plans and submit our plans to Him. Once we make that pledge, and fully submit to Him, He will establish them. He will set them in motion.

This means you should plan in pencil. If we are deeply committed to Him, we must be prepared for the plans to change. A good planner does not like to line through or mark out items in their planner. We have to be prepared to erase and rewrite. Write in pencil and then submit those plans to the Lord. He will let you know when to write them in ink.

I love the way the Message Bible presents it, "Put God in charge of your work, then what you have planned will take place. God made everything with a place and purpose; even the wicked are included—but for judgment."

Go ahead and make those plans. Write them in pencil and just make sure the last item on the task list includes, "Commit these plans to the Lord."

# The Cobbler's Children Have No Shoes

We do not use the word cobbler much these days. A cobbler is a person who mends shoes as a job. Have you stopped in a neighborhood shoe repair shop lately? This saying was coined to refer to a person who is exceptionally good at his profession but is completely unable or unwilling to use this ability to help himself or his own family.

I do words for a living. Ask me for a press release or an internal statement and I can write with the best of them. Press Conference: I am clear, articulate, confident, and intentional. My goal is to make sure that I am clearly understood. After all, I am representing my company. So… why does this wordsmith have such a time with words when it comes to matters of the heart? After all, I am representing myself.

It is easy to write that we need volunteers to help with a community event. It is nearly impossible for me to tell anyone that I need help. It is easy to communicate the needs of the business; it is nearly impossible for me to communicate what I need from others to be my best self.

I can communicate in almost any type of situation, professionally. Today, I am acknowledging that I am not good at communicating with those whom I love the most. They say the first step to changing a behavior is to acknowledge that you have a problem. I want to be able to tell you that I miss you, that I need you, to be able to really tell you that I love you and be equally as certain that you feel my love for you.

Words matter. At a time when it seems like words are all we have… over the phone, over the computer, over Facetime… from a 6-foot distance, I am pleading with all of us, and mostly with myself: Make sure those words are the best you have to offer. Be clear, be open, be honest, and yes, be vulnerable. Use your best words for the people you care about most. Risky, yes. Required? Absolutely.

Proverbs 18:21 (NKJV), "Life and death are in the power of the tongue." The Message Bible makes it REALLY clear: "Words kill, words give life; they are either poison or fruit… you choose."

# Play Cousins

The African American family has some unique roles. There's mama, daddy, sister, brother… and then there is "play" family. Everyone has "play cousins." A play cousin is a friend that you have had for so long that you just treat them like a cousin and call them your cousin. A play cousin can also be the child of your mom or dad's best friend that has been around since childhood.

As society has become more diverse, we no longer live down the street or around the corner from our relatives. Grandma and Grandpa live in another state and our aunts and uncles are scattered about which means our "real cousins" are all over everywhere. Having lived in Atlanta for several decades, a common question was, "Where are you from?" Very few people in Atlanta are actually Atlanta-born and bred. (That is a different story.) With this sociological phenomenon, it is no wonder that an old custom has become a new custom. If you do not live near your family and do not get to see them often, life requires that you quickly develop an extended family. Every working parent household needs a play Grandma who is within a 20-minute radius to step in and help with the kids when someone has a fever and cannot go to school. Play Aunts get put on the pickup list to help get kids from daycare when the traffic is bad. Play Uncles have to stand in sometimes at Daddy-Daughter dances for the single mom.

I grew up as a military dependent. This meant that more often than not, we were in some foreign country – away from family – with other families – who were away from their families. So, we became family to each other. I am amazed that my mom is still close with Aunt Louise from the early 50's when they were stationed overseas together. Play Cousins. Aunt Mary Alice (still fusses at me like I am her own). Play Cousins. The list is awfully long… so much so, that this wonderful Taipei, Taiwan family had a reunion after 50 years. Did I mention, they managed to keep in touch for most of this time with no Internet, no email, and having to pay for long distance calls?

These memories bring me to today. It's my nephew's birthday. He is the son of my Play Sister so that makes me his Play Aunt. I have known him ALL his life, and I have known her most of hers. I directed her wedding when she married a wonderful man, and he became my Play Brother. They are my family. We have shared weddings, births, divorces, the loss of parents, major illness… you name it. It's important to note that having play sisters, brothers, and cousins does not mean you don't have family of your own. It means that in this chaotic, crazy world we live in, there are people who become family by choice. People who are there when you need them… not out of obligation, but out of pure care and concern. It is also PARTICULARLY important to me that ALL of my Play Family, and so extended family… came out of my church family.

Psalm 145:4 (MSG), "Generation after generation stands in awe of your work; each one tells stories of your mighty acts."

# Keeping Company
## [Written During the Pandemic]

Today's thoughts are a bit old school.

Keeping company was the term that was used, back in the day, to refer to people who were courting. Wait, courting is another old reference. Let me rephrase. Keeping company was the way to refer to people who were dating. It really wasn't dating because you likely never left home with the young man. More often than not, keeping company meant that a young lady could invite the appropriately screened young man over to her parent's house – during the daylight- and actually sit with him in the "front room" – alone. All you could basically do was talk to each other and if you were lucky, sneak in a hug or a kiss. Remember we are talking about courting and the rules for courting did not include an option for young ladies to visit young men!

In the dictionary of idioms (it's important to know what these things mean) it says, "Keeping company is to spend time with one for the sake of companionship, or in order to keep them from being lonely." This came to mind as we continue to learn about the impacts of being quarantined or sheltered in place. While people are sheltered, there are concerns about people being alone and being able to cope with the day-to-day impacts of being alone… or not being able to go out and do various things. I spent some time thinking about who I have been "keeping company" with over the past 10 weeks.

I have been intentional in spending time with the Lord. I knew there was value in starting my day with Him... but had gotten to a "random relationship." During this time, I have become extremely focused and intentional in "keeping company" with Him. Talking to Him, listening to Him... and yes, every now and then, feeling the embrace of His care and concern for me. Keeping company with my Savior.

I have been intentional in contacting the people I love and care about. My 80+ year old mom now participates in the Zoom calls and the littles know how to Facetime and will call me out when I am Facetiming them from the car. I have received more cards in the mail during this time than usual … and have learned to host Mastermind and Journal Writing sessions virtually. Keeping company with my family and friends.

I have been intentional in sharing with my neighbors. There are more people outside now than ever before and everyone knows "Bella." We stop and chat, from a distance, with other dog moms and dads, and wave at the other families walking and biking. Keeping company with my neighbors.

Bella and I are great friends. She has learned my moods, and I have definitely learned hers. (She is going to bed at 9PM no matter what you are doing. No good night or anything, she just gets up and goes to bed, and you better not be making noise to disturb her.) Keeping company with my fur baby.

I have been intentional in spending time with myself. Who am I? Who do I want to become? Am I my best self? Am I living my best life? These simple evaluations have allowed me to "keep company" with myself. I like me. I like the person I am and the person I am capable of being. To keep me from being lonely, I read. I write. I nurture my plants and flowers. I plan. I organize. I take pictures. I cook. I clean. I go riding on the freeway with the top down. I work. I work for my employer. I work for myself. I fuel my dreams and passions.

In a time of quarantine and sheltering in place, I kept company. Good company, I might add. It's all a matter of perspective.

Proverbs 13:20 (GNT) – "Keep company with the wise and you will become wise. If you make friends with stupid people, you will be ruined."

Again… the Message Bible makes it really clear:

Proverbs 13:20 (MSG) "Become wise by walking with the wise; hang out with fools and watch your life fall to pieces."

# Virtual Presentations

In our new world order, many of our routine activities are now described as virtual. Virtual meetings, virtual church, virtual happy hours - I recently attended a virtual birthday celebration and am attending a virtual graduation this evening.

I have had virtual staff meetings, virtual doctor visits, virtual family gatherings... all with a strong emphasis on the virtual part. This means that whatever the event is, it is being conducted without the people involved actually getting together – in person. Today, I got an email from Forbes providing, "Best Practices for Virtual Presentations – 15 Expert Tips That Work for Everyone." I would encourage you to read the article.

These virtual events also include virtual presentations. If it is a work meeting, what information is being presented on the screen? It's usually a PowerPoint presentation with lots of graphs and charts. If it is a client meeting, a doctor visit, or a family gathering, there is usually no formal presentation, yet a virtual presentation does in fact take place. Everything others see when they see you is a part of your virtual presentation. I have been in meetings from my office where people have commented on what's on the wall. Last week for a family event, my backdrop included the new flowers on the deck and the lake (which someone noticed is exceptionally low).

Have you thought about what you present when you attend these events? If you are on GoToMeeting, Zoom, WebEx, or even Facetime, everything within the camera view becomes part of your "virtual presentation."

Is there clutter behind you? That impacts your presentation. Are there people walking back and forth behind you? That also impacts your presentation. Are things blurred or in clear view? All these things are part of your virtual presentation.

We spend a lot of time making sure that "we" are camera ready. Lately there is a lot of focus from the top up. Lots of virtual meetings have been conducted with a full face of makeup, hair styled, and a stylish top in the camera view ... with pajama pants and flip flops out of range. The call time for many meetings is literally 10 minutes before the meeting starts, and often that shows in our virtual presentation.

Today, as you prepare for those virtual events on your schedule, take a complete look around. If you are not sure what shows up in the frame, do a video preview on your device, or even better, take a picture. What you see is what they get. More important, is what you see what you really want to present?

Virtual presentations are like first impressions, they stick whether you want them to or not!

2 Timothy 2:15 (NIV), "Do your best to present yourself to God as one approved, a worker who does not need to be ashamed and who correctly handles the word of truth."

# Dying In Service

A critical part of the American holiday known as Memorial Day is the fact that it honors those who have died in service -- specifically, those who have died while serving in the military. This holiday tugs on my heart every year. My dad, Neal A. McQueen, served 27 years active duty in the U.S. Army. It took me a long time to understand the meaning of his service. Not just his service, but the true meaning for ALL who serve. I have learned the importance of thanking those who currently serve, and have served, for their service. My eyes tear up every time I pass through an airport and see soldiers – men and women in camos.

In its simplest form, service is the action of helping or doing work for someone. Carrying that definition through to "military service," it becomes the action of helping or doing work by an individual or group which is part of an army or other militia, whether as a chosen job (volunteer) or as a result of an involuntary draft (conscription). For more context, it can be boiled down to helping or doing work (in a militia) whether you choose or were forced. Fortunately, in the 21st century, conscription no longer exists (maybe it should for some, but that's a topic for a different day). This means that all who are serving today are serving by choice. And you are doing work on behalf of me, a U.S. citizen. Thank you for your service.

Memorial Day is the day set aside to honor the 1.3 million Americans who have lost their lives while serving our country.

That's nearly a million and a half people – some by choice, some not, who have acted on behalf of our country. An action cost them their life. Between 1775 and 1992, more than **six hundred and fifty thousand** of these lives were lost in battle (VA.gov)[4]. Thank you for your service.

This musing is not intended to be somber. It is simply heartfelt. My dad served 27 years. We lived in military communities all my life - on a military base when we were on an overseas assignment, and in a predominantly military community when we lived in off-base housing. This meant everyone that I knew was living the same daily challenge. When all the fathers went to Vietnam, we all watched the nightly news and the updates of the numbers with a sense of trepidation. When we took my dad to Bush Field, it was the first time he was going on assignment without us, and it never crossed my mind that he might not come back. I guess that's how you think in the seventh grade. I am certain, now, that it was a pressing thought on my mother's mind as she was left to be mother and father to four children while he was gone.

Lots of fathers and sons have served. Lots of mothers and daughters have served. For your service in a role that could have cost you your life, I thank you for your service, and today I also thank your families for their sacrifice.

# The Power of Gratitude

It's easy to be grateful. If we pause just long enough to realize that we have the mental capacity to think about what we can or should be grateful for, that's reason enough to be grateful.

More than a few minutes spent thinking about what we have, which we can be grateful for, should easily result in a long list of things. I am alive. I have a reasonable portion of my health and strength (I am grateful for my Church of God In Christ [COGIC] friends who embedded this in my mind). I am clothed in my right mind (at least most of the time). I have shelter, clothing, and food (at least the few snacks that remain). Just thinking of these few things reminded me of the power of gratitude.

There is a song we sing in the Baptist church, "When I think of the goodness of Jesus, and all He has done for me, my soul cries out Hallelujah, thank you for blessing me." Today I am taking modern day liberties and I am doing a remix. Well, at least a rewrite. "When I think of the goodness of Jesus, and all He has done for me, it powers me to thank Him even the more." That is the power of gratitude. Once you start thinking of all that you have to be grateful for, it powers more gratitude. Before I go to sleep at night, I try to record five things that I am grateful for from the day. I keep a gratitude journal and if you read the early entries, they read like Pre-K entries. I wrote the traditional: life, health, strength, shelter, food... the superficial stuff. As I read through later entries, I see more and more the power of gratitude.

Gratitude helps you grow-- in your relationship with God, in your relationship with others, and even in your relationship with yourself. It teaches you what matters. It's the power of gratitude.

Being grateful for what God provides is easy. Being grateful for ALL He prevented is even more powerful. Being grateful for the people in your life – Mama'em, (Southern for Mama and them), children, and friends. Easy. Being grateful for those you have loved AND lost is powerful. I am grateful for the memories and lives well lived.

Being grateful for what you do have, check. But have you ever stopped to be grateful for what you do not have? Being grateful for lack builds your faith. It is my chance to be grateful that I have a loving Father who not only wants the best for me, but also knows what is best for me… and when. I am grateful that lack builds my trust that HE will provide. My lack is His covering me in ways I cannot imagine or understand. And I am grateful that I do not have to worry or ponder about these things.

Each small thing, whether good or bad, is reason to be grateful. That's the power of gratitude.

1 Thessalonians 5:18 (KJV), "In everything give thanks: for this is the will of God in Christ Jesus concerning you."

The same passage in the Message translation, v16-18, "Be cheerful no matter what; pray all the time; thank God no matter what happens. This is the way God wants you who belong to Christ Jesus to live."

# *Long. Personal. Controversial*

"Injustice anywhere is a threat to justice everywhere. We are caught in an inescapable network of mutuality, tied in a single garment of destiny. Whatever affects one directly, affects all indirectly." — Martin Luther King Jr., American Baptist minister. Excerpt from his letter from the Birmingham Jail. April 16, 1963.

"Injustice anywhere is a threat to justice everywhere. We are caught in an inescapable network of mutuality, tied in a single garment of destiny. Whatever affects one directly, affects all indirectly." — Martin Luther King Jr., Replay from a Minneapolis Street. May 25, 2020.

Mutuality is the foundation of human existence. It is the sharing of a feeling, action, or relationship between two or more parties. Mutuality is inescapable if you watch the video of George Floyd, the 46-year-old African American man who was murdered by a police officer in Minneapolis, Minnesota on May 25, 2020, for allegedly using a counterfeit twenty-dollar bill in a convenience store.

21st century media makes it "inescapable." In every medium, on every platform, the horrible video of this situation is inescapable. The reality of the situation is inescapable. The mutuality of the situation is inescapable. Thank God for the cameras from the nearby stores. Thank God for the people on the street, who begged and pleaded and made sure these images were captured.

George Floyd. Handcuffed. On the ground. Four and half minutes... becomes lifeless. Nine minutes and 29 seconds total. "Please, I can't breathe." George Floyd. "Whatever affects one directly, affects all indirectly." -Martin Luther King, Jr.

In May 2020, an incident occurred in Minneapolis, MN involving George Floyd and a police officer.

At the time of writing this in 2020, the motto of the Minneapolis Police Department, which was directly from their webpage at the time, read: "To protect with courage. To serve with compassion."

If the video of this situation was a demonstration of protecting with courage and serving with compassion, we are all at risk.

The mutuality of this entire incident is profound:

Executed at the hands of people who have long felt superior.

Executed at the hands of people who have had their "knees on our necks" in every way possible for as long as can be remembered.

Executed initially in clandestine ways, executed today under the guise of protecting and serving.

Where is the protection and compassion for a man, who – according to all video accounts - never resisted, never showed any signs of force, was unarmed, was handcuffed upon removal from his vehicle, and was placed face down on the ground?

Still handcuffed, and in visible signs of distress, he manages to say PLEASE as he begs for breath and becomes listless after nearly four minutes. You continue to place the full force of your body, the body called to protect and serve (we won't talk about the courage and compassion parts of that motto) the full force of your body… on his neck.

Nine long minutes and 29 seconds longer.

I am affected. I am African American. I have sons, I have nephews, and I have cousins. I know African American men who look like George Floyd.

Whatever affects one directly. I am affected.

**"Injustice anywhere is a threat to justice everywhere**. We are caught in an inescapable network of mutuality, tied in a single garment of destiny. Whatever affects one directly, affects all indirectly." — Martin Luther King Jr., Replay from my daily life.

When you visit their webpage at the time of this book's publication, that motto is no longer visible. What is present is, "We in the Minneapolis Police Department gain our authority from the community. We recognize that public safety is not just the absence of crime but the presence of justice," (Minneapolismn.gov).[5]

# Long and Still Personal - Knees

When I knelt to pray this morning, I was overwhelmed. So overwhelmed that I ended up prostrate on the floor. My prayers often start with the phrase… "As I kneel down before you…" and as I said those words this morning, the burden of knees and kneeling was just too much. I immediately thought of the times I have knelt to pray and the pressure of my own weight on the floor was too much.

Knees have become controversial.

The symbolism of knees in my life has changed dramatically. One of my earliest memories is the phrase… "take a knee." Joe Olliff and Guesner Cannon, football coaches at Glenn Hills High School, taught the basics of football to the varsity cheerleaders. The goal was simple – to make sure that we knew the basics of the game well enough to know when and how to support the players on the field – when to cheer. I am grateful for those lessons. I am one of four girls, so there was not much football in my home. Not only did these basics help me understand the game, it fueled my love of the game. Taking a knee in football temporarily stops the game. Sometimes it occurs after the snap to stop the clock… but the most meaningful use for me was when someone on the field was injured. WE ALL TOOK A KNEE. Both teams, everyone who was standing, took a knee. Helmets off, heads bowed, in respect for the injured player on the field– the injured person.

Another symbolism. "Taking a knee" is used in the military. My dad was a career military man and I lived in military settings ALL of my life. In the military, taking a knee is a sign of respect. It means taking a breather or taking a rest while on a mission. It can also be used to mean that you are pausing and stepping back to consider a situation. By no means is it a disrespectful gesture. In fact, you will often see soldiers take a knee at the foot of a fallen friend's grave. It is the ultimate sign of respect for a friend.

Back to football. In recent years, taking a knee in sports has been used as a sign of protest. The purpose of the protest has not always been clear, but to kneel when everyone else was "standing" became an obvious symbol of disagreement and disrespect. We are still in the midst of that discussion.

Today, my faith, my hope, my belief, and my foundation is God. I kneel before Him daily as the sovereign being in my life. I kneel before Him as a sign of respect. I kneel because He is who gives me life and breath. He is the air I breathe. I kneel in awe and reverence. I kneel to protest the sins of the world… mine first and all others. I kneel and pray.

George Floyd took a knee…

Not willingly, and not as a sign of respect to the injured.

He was the injured.

George Floyd took a knee…

Not as a pause to reconsider the situation.

He was the situation.

George Floyd took a knee…

Not as a breather, it cost him his breath.

George Floyd took a knee…

Not as a sign of protest…

> He humbly protested,
>
> "Please, I can't breathe."

Scripture teaches in Romans 14:11 (NLT), "As surely as I live, says the Lord, every knee will bow before me; every tongue will acknowledge God."

The Message Bible translation says it loud and clear: Same chapter, same verses:

Romans 14:11-12 (MSG), [10-12] "So where does that leave you when you criticize a brother? And where does that leave you when you condescend to a sister? I would say it leaves you looking pretty silly—or worse. Eventually, we are all going to end up kneeling side by side in the place of judgment, facing God. Your critical and condescending ways are not going to improve your position there one bit." Read it for yourself in scripture: "As I live and breathe," God says, "every knee will bow before me; Every tongue will tell the honest truth that I and only I am God."

Footnote: I usually end my morning devotional with music. Today, the song God placed on my heart was "City on Our Knees" by TobyMac. Head over to YouTube and listen when you get a moment. (YouTube.com)[6]

# Love Hurts

There is a fairly popular song that opens with the words "love hurts." It is currently being used as the opener for an Aspercreme® commercial. (Now you know what gets my attention.)

Until recently, I never knew, or really cared, what the rest of the words to the song were. For most of us, the focus of love in our lives is always on the good feelings: the romantic, the gushy feelings, the "everything's rosy" kind of stuff. Why? Because that is what the commercials and the advertisements show us. They help create and fuel this perception that everything, or at least most things, about love are good and positive. It is not just the commercials and ads; in the best chick flicks girl meets boy, girl and boy fall in love… and live happily ever after.

Before any further words are put to paper, I am issuing a disclaimer: I am not anti-love. When I think about the sanctity of love when it exists the way God intended it to be, it is indeed a beautiful thing. There are just three problems: the two people in the love equation and the collective inability to allow love to exist the way God intended it to be.

It is the 21st century and the days of young ladies dreaming about the love of their life are gone. If there is any dreaming going on, I can assure you it looks quite different. Love in the 21st century is conditional. I love you if you are tall enough or have the right car and the right job. I love you if you do the right things for me – right as in what I want and not usually what I need. I love you as long as things as going well. I love you as long as there is no work involved in keeping the love alive. All these conditions and stipulations are the reason… love hurts.

We do not deliver these conditions and stipulations when we first meet. That is a pretty dangerous situation by itself. When we first meet, we are doing whatever it takes to impress the other person, whether it has anything to do with our authentic selves or not. The aim is the win, not the keep. I remembered, much too late, my dad used to say, "Whatever you do to get them, it takes that and three times more to keep them." Those long "I don't want to hang up" phone calls have to become long intimate conversations that go deep into the night. Those "can't stand to be away from you moments" have to become you laying on the floor at my feet while I nurse the baby at 2am. Those "ride or die sentiments" have to come to life when my dream job is in another state… and I need you to "ride" with me.

Love hurts. Not always because people intend to, but more often because we forget to make sure love is a lifelong journey. It is a noun when used to describe a thing, but it has to be a verb in order to survive. It has to be a modified verb to thrive, modified by words like relentless and reckless, like unconditional and incomparable. It has to be forgiving, daily long-suffering, always and forever abiding. Yes, these are tall orders – heavy standards— but when they are not met, love hurts.

It is more than ironic that the greatest illustration of love that we have is a very painful one. Just look at the cross— unyielding love.

I finally looked up the rest of the words to the song, Love Hurts.

In case you are wondering, the song was released by a group called Nazareth in 1994 on an album called *Hair of the Dog*. All of the words in the previous sentence are food for thought.

# Long. Personal. Sad.

One of my coping mechanisms is to avoid dwelling on things that I cannot change. On the surface, it means things like rain, broken glass, or bad traffic... everyday events. Age and maturity have taught me that dwelling on these things, lingering over how they make me feel... does me no good. Accept what is, and let it go.

Accepting does not mean that I don't think of things that I can do better the next time: keep an umbrella in my office AND the car in case of rain, don't carry glasses with too many things in my hand in case I drop something, and leave the office after the normal quitting time in case rush hour was bad.

Dwelling is an odd word, really. I do words for a living. In "doing words," it is essential that I know how, and when, to use them in context. Like many words, dwell can be a verb or a noun. As a verb, it is used without an object and means to live or stay as a permanent resident – to reside. But we don't go around today asking people where they "dwell." It can also mean to live or continue in a given condition or state, as in "to dwell in happiness." It also means to linger over, emphasize, or ponder in thought, speech, or writing (often followed by *on* or *upon*), as in "to dwell on the current conditions of our world," (Dictionary. com, 2020).[7] This is where I got stuck.

I do not want to dwell on the current conditions of our world. I do not want to live in a world that permanently looks and feels like this. I do not want to stay in this space as a permanent resident. All around me, it feels like we are being forced to accept senseless death. In 2020, this meant millions of people lost their lives due to a virus. Senseless because too many people would not heed the guidance and precautions that have been issued on ways to stop the spread of a deadly pandemic. Senseless because the needed supplies and materials were not readily available and in too many cases, the cost of these supplies became egregious. At the same time, I do not want to live or continue in this as a condition or state. I do not want to dwell in quarantine. I do not want to dwell in physical distancing… as a state of being. Senseless death continues as we experience school shootings and mass shootings in record numbers across society.

Most of all, I do not want to dwell; I do not want to linger over, emphasize, or ponder in thought, speech or writing the loss of life, liberty, and the pursuit of happiness. There it is again, the loss of life.

And the cycle starts all over. I do not want to be a permanent resident of a society where the loss of life can be easily captured on the latest iPhone, where a limited value of life is a permanent condition. Yet, I am forced to linger over, emphasize, and ponder, in all of my thoughts, in my speech, and here in my writing, everything that is going on around me. There are things I cannot change. While the realization that I cannot change them is ever present, I know that accepting them is also not an option.

I went to my place of peace this morning and found these words in Psalm 133 (NKJV), "Behold, how good and how pleasant *it is* For brethren to **dwell** together in unity! *It is* like the precious oil upon the head, running down on the beard, the beard of Aaron,

Running down on the edge of his garments. *It is* like the dew of Hermon, Descending upon the mountains of Zion; For there the Lord commanded the blessing— Life forevermore."

I challenge you to take each of the definitions of the word dwell and to insert them in this scripture every time you read it. Replace the word dwell with one of the definitions:

… for brethren to ~~dwell~~ (live or stay as a permanent resident; reside) in unity.

… for brethren to ~~dwell~~ (live or continue in a given condition or state) in unity.

… for brethren to ~~dwell~~ (linger over, emphasize, or ponder in thought, speech, or writing) in unity. May your dwelling bring you peace.

# Still Personal - Pausing

I started sharing my musings publicly when God spoke to me (and gave Latrese Holloway words that confirmed it) that the messages He was sharing with me were not just for me.

I often asked… then for whom, Lord? His response was loud and clear. Knowing who is my job. Your job is to record and share without question. And so, I am. That means that many of my musings are personal.

I have always been a recorder. Journaling is just a form of recording. Not just a litany of the day, but thoughts, hopes, and dreams… and for me, what thus saith the Lord. I write every day. I have for years. In fact, every day I try to read my journal entry from the previous year and with the entry of a new decade, I have been reading the journal entry from the previous decade.

Wow. Think back to May 2010. Barack Obama was President—don't need to say much more.

Personally, in May 2010, my dad was still with us. Slipping away slowly … but still there. My personal and professional life was completely different in 2010. In 2010, I had a spouse, was supporting children in college and had just started my dream job. (Look where He brought me from!)

When I originally wrote this in 2020, there was so much going on around me. Most of it was not good. I spent a great deal of time dwelling on that over a period of several days.

Despite the intensity and escalation of many of the events, I took time to pause.

Musing has taught me a lot about myself. In learning myself, I am better able to teach others.

As I thought about taking time to pause today, a Sunday, I was reminded of the true meaning of sabbath. The Scripps National Spelling Bee has taught me to start with the origin of the word before seeking to understand its meaning. The origin of the Hebrew sabbat – represented as [t'B;v] - is uncertain, but it seems to have derived from the verb sabat, meaning to stop, to cease, or to keep. Its theological meaning is rooted in God's rest following the six days of creation (Gen. 2:2-3). The Greek noun sabbat [savbbaton] translates the Hebrew noun sabbat- represented as [t'B;v]. The noun form is used primarily to denote the seventh day of the week, though it may occasionally refer to the Sabbath week (Lev 23:15-16).

Today I am taking a rest. I am taking a sabbath--taking time to rest my mind, body, and spirit. Some will say I am keeping sabbath. Resting. Pausing.

# *Month End*

Today, I am pausing to say Happy Birthday to my sister Phyllis, also known as Pegless. She is the comedian in our family and keeps us all laughing. Pegless… it is your day.

Today, I am pausing to close out the month… it is the end of May, the traditional start of summer with plans for picnics, cookouts, reunions, beaches, and theme parks fully solidified. Well, that is what it used to mean.

Today, I am pausing: It is the time when I look back at my goals for the month and the quarter and reassess where I am and where I need to be going.

Today, I am pausing to reflect on what is ahead, and realizing that I do not know what is ahead.

Taking a rest. Keeping sabbath. What I know for sure, God is in control--in control of all that has happened, all that is happening, and all that will happen. He has a purpose and a plan… neither of which come with guarantees that there will not be any pain, any heartache, any anger, or any frustration. The only guarantee that we can have in any of this is His Word.

"Rest is important to your spiritual walk with the Lord, and many Christians today don't appreciate the value of rest or keeping the Sabbath day holy. Rest allows our mind, body, and soul to renew and start with even more strength and focus. Scripture is filled with **God's promises** (emphasis added) to provide rest when we seek Him" (BibleStudyTools.com).[8]

# When Least Becomes Most

It is another word morning for me. I have spent a lot of time lately trying to find the right words for the right situations. I love words and the irony of them. I do words for a living.

It is the start of a new month and when this month ends, we will be at the end of the second quarter. It is really hard to believe that nearly half of the year is gone. For the planner in me, that means I need to start looking at my yearly goals and my quarterly goals, to see where I am, and to probably kick things up a notch.

When I take time to review my goals and when I am completely honest with myself about where I am, I have to consider the effort I have put in towards the goal. Is it just something that I wrote down or something that I actually committed to AND worked on? Notice that the AND is emphasized. You have to be committed AND do the work. They go together. Trust me, when you do something you are not committed to, your work is shoddy and haphazard. You really do not care about the outcome; you just want it done. But when you are committed – you care as much about the work as the outcome.

Two of my favorite authors have recently motivated me in this area. Hal Elrod, author of "Miracle Mornings" and "The Miracle Equation," teaches: "Solidify your extraordinary effort and make your goal inevitable by committing to your process without being emotionally attached to your results." Commit to and stay the course even when you do not feel like it is working. Another favorite, B.J. Fogg, says in his book, "Tiny

Habits," "No behavior happens without a prompt. Prompts are the cues that remind us to act."

My initial thought with most things centers around what it will take. What level of commitment and what level of effort? These thoughts often get in the way of me doing anything. When I think of "Tiny Habits" (which is, by the way, a great book), I am reminded of the words "least" and "most." Both words can be used as adverbs, nouns, or adjectives. Where they have their root, and their most meaning is when used to describe extent. As an adverb, they can both be used to indicate how much effort, how much position, or how much importance exists in the situation.

You should try to do better. That is the least you can do, which means that it is the smallest effort you can make towards being better.

You should try to do better. That is the most you can do, which means that is the greatest effort you can make towards being better.

Doing a small amount becomes a greater amount.

A small word of encouragement becomes the greatest motivation.

A small word of prayer becomes the most inspiration.

That is when least becomes most.

Matthew 13:32 (KJV)

"Which indeed is the least of all seeds: but when it is grown, it is the greatest among herbs, and becometh a tree, so that the birds of the air come and lodge in the branches thereof. smallest effort becomes the greatest impact."

# *In My Feelings*

I cannot shake this feeling. I cannot shake **these** feelings. There are definitely more than one--some that I cannot even name.

Morning prayer with Pastor Quincy Stratford reminded me that I need to be led by faith and not my feelings. My initial thought was… yes, but I cannot feel my faith. That is when I really knew what the message for today was. I cannot be guided by my feelings… at least not in the things that matter. Things do not go well when I am "in my feelings."

I feel like I need to buy something every time I get an email from Nordstrom. In my feelings.

I feel like I am really going to start eating healthy and go Tabitha Brown vegan every time I am in Whole Foods. In my feelings.

I feel like I am ready to do a marathon every time I hit the pavement. In my feelings.

I feel like people should understand and be more caring. In my feelings.

I feel like these things should NOT keep happening. In my feelings.

I feel like I am in the midst of chaos. In my feelings.

My feelings will create behaviors and outcomes that are not good for me. I have evidence of that ALL around me: Too many clothes (I unsubscribed from Nordstrom's email in the middle of this message!). So many projects that are in various stages of completion. Feelings can lead to more feelings that we do not want, creating a vicious cycle.

But, when I look around me with a more discerning eye, even though I cannot feel my faith in the midst of things, I KNOW it exists. The evidence of my faith is overwhelming. I would not be who I am and where I am without it. When I am in my feelings, I am all in ME. When I am in my faith, I have to be all in Him.

Please be assured, we are all entitled to feel the way we feel. It is letting those feelings guide, direct, and determine our actions that causes the problems. Our actions and behaviors have to be guided by faith, not feelings.

I cannot see faith and most often, do not feel it… but I have a promise: "Now faith is confidence in what we hope for and assurance about what we do not see," Hebrews 11:1 (NIV).

# In My Language

I have a dear friend, who says to me often, "Par moi je pense que tu es jolie." (Translation: By me, I think you are pretty.)

Let's be clear. My friend is a 6'5", 300-pound African American male. At first glance, you would not think French, but he speaks several languages fluently and often intersperses other languages into our conversations.

At first, I felt intimidated because even though English is my native language, I often struggle to speak English well, and I have had several failed attempts to undertake learning Japanese, Spanish, and French. No Rosetta Stone certificates for me.

As I have spent time trying to wade through the various messages that people send, verbally and visually, I realized that we all have our own language. I have a well-known fondness for the Scripps Spelling Bee, and I get excited when the students ask for the country of origin and the root of the word. Increasingly, I am learning how the origin of a word and the root of the word influence the meaning.

I work in the beverage industry. We call it the NARTD industry... the non-alcoholic ready-to-drink industry--also known as soft drinks. Ever wondered why they are called soft drinks?

A soft drink is a drink that usually contains carbonated water (although some lemonades are not carbonated), a sweetener, and a natural or artificial flavoring. Soft drinks are called 'soft' in contrast with 'hard' alcoholic drinks.

Yet, based on the country (or state of origin), these beverages are called pop or soda. According to various internet sources, soft drinks were called pop because of the sound made when you remove the cork from the bottle. Fast forward to the 21$^{st}$ century, and you would think "pop" would have been replaced as soft drinks now come in PET bottles with resealable caps. And then there is soda. Many attribute this term to the British. It was derived from early formulas that combined water with pressurized carbon dioxide gas. In today's commercial market, sodium bicarbonate is no longer used in the product's manufacture, yet the term "soda" has remained attached to the name for drinks made from carbonated water.

What does this have to do with anything? What messages you hear are calibrated by the language you speak. Something as simple as water can mean anything from Dasani to smartwater to Perrier to Brita filtered water to plain old tap water. It all depends on your place of origin.

As we filter out the myriad of messages being sent today, consider the language in which it was spoken. It took a while for me to be comfortable with the various French, Italian, and German phrases spoken by my friend, but asking for meaning is how I learned to understand.

Having just celebrated Pentecost ... very fitting reminder.

Genesis 11:1-9 (NIV)

"Now the whole world had one language and a common speech. As people moved eastward, they found a plain in Shinar and settled there. They said to each other, "Come, let's make bricks and bake them thoroughly." They used brick instead of stone, and tar for mortar. Then they said, "Come, let us build ourselves a city, with a tower that reaches to the heavens, so that we may make a name for ourselves; otherwise, we will be scattered over the face of the whole earth."

But the Lord came down to see the city and the tower the people were building. The Lord said, "If as one people speaking the same language, they have begun to do this, then nothing they plan to do will be impossible for them. Come, let us go down and confuse their language so they will not understand each other."

So the Lord scattered them from there over all the earth, and they stopped building the city. That is why it was called Babel— because there the Lord confused the language of the whole world. From there the Lord scattered them over the face of the whole earth.

# Storm Warning

I often use the phrase, "You are either in a storm, coming out of a storm, or preparing for one." It is called life.

The official hurricane season for the Atlantic Basin (the Atlantic Ocean, the Caribbean Sea, and the Gulf of Mexico) is from June 1st to November 30th. According to the National Hurricane Center, the peak of the season is from mid-August to late October.[9] If you live anywhere near these areas, you quickly learn the routine of preparing for hurricane season. There is a very finite list of things that you are encouraged to have on hand: Basics like bottled water and canned food. Flashlights and batteries. All of these things are on the lists issued by the National Hurricane Center each year. (Notice, the list does not include toilet paper.)

What are not on the lists are the other set of essentials that people share with you when they learn you are new to hurricane preparation. Things like, fill all your bathtubs with water. No one wants to use Dasani to flush the toilet. Learn how to drain your pool. There will be enough flooding without your pool spilling over. Bring inside any and everything that can take flight, early. And, most importantly, put all your valuable papers in a plastic bag and keep it high.

The contrast between these two versions of preparation guidance is very telling. The first is very clinical–an almost common-sense list if you understand what a hurricane really is. Hurricanes are large, swirling storms with violent winds. (I did notice that most formal definitions did not mention rain.) Truth be told, these are probably emergency supplies every household should have on hand for any situation. The second list comes from the experience of having been in a hurricane and having those aha moments that come from the struggle to survive.

Storms are a full-time business. We get lots of predictions. In fact, by June of 2020, there were already three named storms on the list. Speaking of the list, tropical storms are given names when they display a rotating circulation pattern and wind speeds of 39 miles per hour (63 kilometers per hour). A tropical storm develops into a hurricane when wind speeds reach 74 mph (119 kph). Lists of hurricane names have been developed for many of the major ocean basins around the world. Today, there are six lists of hurricane names in use for Atlantic Ocean and Eastern North Pacific storms. These lists rotate, one each year. That means the list of this year's hurricane names for each basin will come up again six years from now.

Life is also full-time business. If my phrase is correct, then why don't we prepare for life's storms the same way we prepare for hurricane season? Why don't we stock up on funds so when the financial storm comes, we are prepared? Why don't we spend more time with our children when they are young so when the puberty storm hits, we are better prepared to deal with them? We never recite the 102 scriptures in the Bible on healing until the health storm arises.

Tropical storms are the initial display of the hurricane that results when wind speeds increase. It can also feel like a hurricane when car issues, the water heater issues, and the cell phone issues happen all at the same time.

Just as with hurricane season preparations, there is no step to take to prevent the storm. The focus is on being ready when the storm comes. Notice, not "if," but when.

Scripture teaches us that in this life we will have tribulations (storms). It also offers us the best preparation there is—" in me [Jesus] you may have peace.

John 16:33 (ESV) says, "I have said these things to you, that in me you may have peace. In the world you will have tribulation. But take heart; I have overcome the world."

Back to the weather report.

*Prelude.* This isn't the musing, it is the prelude to the musing. A prelude is an introduction to something more important. But there are some thoughts that I just had to get out. Think of it as the music that plays just before the song really starts.

Be careful what you ask for. I have always wanted to write a book and to be an author. Somehow being an author seemed like an honorable thing. When my besties and I read "Write It Down, Make It Happen: Knowing What You Want And Getting It" by Henriette Anne Klauser," 20 years ago, I wrote it down, along with 99 other random things. Life happened and the idea of being an author waned… especially after working on my dissertation. That will kill any desire to write anything ever again. I somehow got back in the saddle and began writing again after school—writing for me and about me. Hold on, the musing is coming. Just like with "Write It Down, Make It Happen," I read another awesome book, "Your 100 Day Prayer" by John I. Snyder (I know, I talk about this book ALL of the time as it is truly life-changing.) The book opens by asking you to commit to praying for 100 days – "praying on and for" something for 100 days. Each day, you bring your issue before God in prayer. Using this during my morning devotion, after Scripture, a brief reading, and prayer, there is a place in Snyder's book for you to record thoughts, notes, or insights as God reveals them to you, and so musings were born. Now, for today's musing.

# Boldness

My generation did not treat boldness as a positive attribute. Boldness meant brassy. Bold meant loud and close to obnoxious. That was back when I really did not have a relationship with God, or at least not like the one I have now. I did not know that the Scripture teaches us to come "boldly" to the throne of grace (Hebrews 4:16). Keep reading. Or at least, I kept reading. I read some work by Dave Ramsey, and he introduced me to the concept of a BHAG. The BHAG idea comes from a book by Jim Collins- "From Good to Great." READING IS FUNDAMENTAL.

A BHAG is a Big, Hairy, Audacious, Goal. One so big, that you know it is going to take divine intervention to reach. After reading about it, I listened to a great audio version which made it even clearer. (Dave's goal was to run a marathon.)

I have spent a good portion of my life, probably most of my life, setting goals. Writing down the things I wanted (or so I thought) out of life. I learned about SMART goals… to make sure they were Specific, Measurable, Attainable, Realistic, and Time-bound. Wait, realistic. That is where I got off track. Realistic is what I think I can achieve on my own. Bold is what I can I achieve with God's help. Snyder reminded me of this when he wrote, "The reality of the resurrection isn't only an encouragement just for the end of the world. It is supposed to affect everything that we think about and do today. The same power that operated to raise Jesus' physical body from the tomb on Easter morning is operating this very day to bring dead things back to life: dead dreams, dead careers, dead marriages, and all the rest. This good news is at the heart of faith – don't forget it." (It's on Day 66 on p.143 if you have the book.)

PRAISE BREAK!

My dead goal of being an author has been resurrected. It is now my BHAG. The book you are holding was my BHAG!

Hebrews 4:16 (MSG), "So let's walk right up to him and get what he is so ready to give. Take the mercy, accept the help."

# Trusted With the Challenge

"What next, Lord?" This is often our thought when there are a lot of things going on at the same time; usually not good things, or challenges.

Challenges are those things in life that seem to test our abilities, like a physical challenge. Push-ups are a challenge for me. Situations also challenge us—things like a child with an unexpected fever on the morning of your final presentation, or an adult suddenly faced with unemployment. The key to most challenges lies in the "ability" to deal with them. Most responsible adults immediately start trying to think of and sort out options. Can I get the child in to see the doctor today? Who can I call to keep the child? What might be causing the fever? How much money is in the savings account? Is my resume current? Options. As soon as the challenge presents itself, we use our ability to reason and plan to come up with options: our ability.

Our ability in a challenge is often the source of the angst. Our ability is never fully adequate for the situation. If it was, there would be no real challenge. Child sick? Husband at home during the day? Not a challenge (or at least shouldn't be). Unemployed? But you completed Step 3 of Dave Ramsey's plan?. Not a challenge (for at least 3-6 months). When we have an immediate solution, we have to remind ourselves, this is an inconvenience, not a challenge. We have become a society where any little bit of disruption sends us spinning. Anything not on our plan or our self-generated agenda becomes an issue.

Today, I pause to give respect to the real challenges of life.

Poverty. We have double digit unemployment in our country. For many, unemployment now means no job, and little hope of finding a job. That is a challenge.

Chronic illness. Our health care system is broken. So broken, that many who need care for a chronic illness (defined as one that WILL NOT go away and likely requires daily attention) cannot obtain the health care services that could mean life or death. That is a challenge. The list of REAL challenges goes on: educational system issues, literacy issues, drug-related issues… you name it.

What is more important than the inconvenience or the challenge is knowing, with absolute certainty, Who has the most ability in handling the situation. In the traditional Southern Baptist Church, we used to sing a song, with the words" … "surely, my God is able to a carry you through."

That is why we can be trusted with the challenges. We know Who is able.

# Taking Chances

Many think taking chances is dangerous. But is it always? Of course, pulling out in front of that tractor trailer on the highway is taking a chance. Driving a small, twenty-five-year-old car, chances when pulling out in front the tractor trailer, not good. Driving a brand-new Bugatti Chiron with over 1400 bhp, chances are excellent! (Not likely due to its $3.4M price tag, but excellent chances nonetheless).

In the simplest definition, taking a chance means to do something that is risky or dangerous. Just the inclusion of the words risky and dangerous suggests that taking a chance is not a good thing. But, if we take a closer look, everything in life, all of our everyday goings and comings, have the potential to be risky or dangerous. If you drive to work every day in most major cities, there is a pretty high risk of being in a traffic accident.  If you stay at home to avoid the traffic, in many of these same cities, there is the risk of someone breaking into your home. If you stand, you are taking a chance that you might fall. If you sit (too long), it may be dangerous to your circulation. All of these considerations show us that in fact, life is a game of chance.

Life involves people. So, in the life game of chance, we are often in a position to take chances on people. Now, the stakes are different. There is an element of free will that exists in taking chances on people that does exist with the other chances in life. There is no one in the "traffic chance" who says, "Let me go out and see who I can get in an accident with today." Taking a chance on a living, breathing, fallible human being is a completely different story. In these chance-taking situations, there are a lot of variables.

To take a chance on someone is to give someone an opportunity to succeed when there is an appreciable risk that they may fail or result in a negative outcome. This is NOT about setting someone up to fail. This is NOT about creating an increased risk of a negative outcome. Taking a chance on someone is actually giving them the faith and encouragement needed to try regardless of outcome. When someone is there for you, it is so much easier to step out, to try, and to give it your best. Taking a chance on someone says I believe in you. Not, I believe in the outcome, but I believe in your effort. Having someone believe in your effort is the ultimate gift. In my humble way of thinking, having someone believe in your effort is the magic to being successful. Having someone take a chance on me, means that my odds of succeeding have just gone up. My faith is bolstered by your faith in me.

Today, hearing "I got you" meant I get to take a chance on my dreams.

Taking chances is definitely a faith walk. Taking chances on someone is an act of love.

# "The Revolution Will Not Be Televised"

This is the title of a song. It is a poem written by Gil Scott-Heron, first performed in 1970. MORE THAN FIFTY YEARS AGO.

It is a powerful statement about our inability to sit back and think that the changes needed (the revolution) would come to us, live and in living color – through the wonders of television. I am not sure why I listened to this oldie last Friday night, but I am sure there was meaning in what I heard.

I heard words that sounded so very true for today. With unprecedented events happening all around us, we cannot expect to sit idly by and watch things unfold like a Netflix miniseries where someone has documented information to present to us. The change that we are loudly demanding… change in healthcare, change in access to a living-wage, not a minimum wage, change in the treatment of people – all colors, all ages, all genders, all heights… ALL PEOPLE, that change.

That change is not going to happen because we demand it. It is not going to happen as the result of brute force or police batons. It will not happen as the result of a legal mandate. Things will not change ONLY because we gather and protest. And they certainly will not change with a flick of the remote.

Even though the revolution will not be televised, we still have to make sure there is one. In a lot of ways, it feels like we are in fact watching reruns. The same images, the same script. Fifty years later...

Too many times, activities are conducted for the pleasure of the viewing audience.

Not this time. The revolution will not be televised, but that does not mean the show has been cancelled. It means we have to be the show. We have to do to the work that shows who we are—the work that makes us the people we need to be. Person by person. The work that shows we do want change, and the work that shows we will have those awkward conversations; we will have those direct engagements. the work that shows we are committed, we are in it for the long haul... even when it does not seem productive, and YES... even when no one is watching.

I have put Gil Scott-Heron on repeat. (Not in front of the children).

# Relationship Goals

Relationships are hard. Relationships with people are hard. Relationships with people are hard because people have emotions. Relationships are emotional. Relationships require work.

I have family and friends—loved ones. Most of my family relationships are not by choice. What I mean is, you are born into a family... so you get what you get. You do not exactly go around saying, I want a sister or a brother and consciously work to build a relationship with someone as your sibling. It is important to note that sometimes even with accepting "you got what you got" the relationships among family can be strained and estranged. Relationships are hard.

I do have some family relationships that are by choice. When you get married, you are not just choosing a spouse; they come with accessories: family. Trust me, it is definitely a choice to be in relationship with your in-law family. Again, there are some that are absolutely amazing (whew!) and then others best loved from a distance.

Speaking of choice, most of our friend relationships are purely choice. You meet someone, you realize you have things in common, and you become friends. You choose to be friends and you choose what the friendship is going to look like. Some folks become inseparable, and others can go months without seeing each other or talking... and then pick back up as if it were yesterday.

In doing some work recently on "relationship goals," I realized several things about myself. I have 3.5 really good friends. By my definition, "really good friends" means we have been through the darkest of times together and are still able to be friends. Dark times include health issues, loss of loved ones, extreme hurt, financial loss… the kind of stuff that can really take you out. These friends' status is what is  now called "ride or die." These are the friends that I saw when I woke up from surgery and the ones that held my eye at my dad's funeral. This was never the relationship goal. The goal was to be friendly, to have someone to hang out with, go shopping, and do girl stuff with. The reality is, we all have lives. We have jobs, careers, spouses, children, elderly parents, pets, and oh… other friends. This means that sometimes friends get put on the back burner. That is not the goal, or the desire… it is called life.

I value these 3.5 relationships. 2 of the 3.5, I met at church. We share the value of a deep personal relationship with God. I actually believe this is the foundation that has allowed us to be friends for over 30 years. I am daily grateful for them and their presence in my life.

I am sure by now; you are wondering about the other one point five really good friends. It is a long story, but that is why I have relationship goals. Not past tense, but active. Goals… things I am working on every day. The one point five are best loved from afar. A critical part of relationships is accepting what is.

I like you, because. I love you, although.

Relationships are hard. Relationships with people are hard. Relationships are emotional.

John 15:13 (NIV), "Greater love has no one than this: to lay down one's life for one's friends.

Hebrews 10:24-25 (GNV), "And let us consider one another, to provoke unto love, and to good works, Not forsaking the fellowship that we have among ourselves, as the manner of some is: but let us exhort one another..."

Hebrews 10:24-25 (NIV), "And let us consider how we may spur one another on toward love and good deeds, not giving up meeting together, as some are in the habit of doing, but encouraging one another-and all the more as you see the Day approaching."

1 Peter 5:6-7; Ephesians 4:2-3; Proverbs 31:10-11; Exodus 20:12

# The Gospel According to Johnny

I am choosing to present this as an advantage instead of a chore in case Bella decides to read this. Interesting things happen along our daily walks as Bella searches diligently and earnestly for the perfect spot to do her business.

That is how we met Johnny. Johnny is a precious 4-year-old who lives near me. When we first moved to the neighborhood, we would see Johnny and his mom in the yard and he was only interested in Bella. "What's her name?" he asked, almost every day. After a while, he remembered her name and began asking, "Where did she come from?" Not sure what prompted the question, but it gave me an opportunity to talk about rescuing her from some bad people. He kindly told me that was a nice thing to do.

We generally see Johnny and his mom every day… or at least every day that I am on schedule and Bella is cooperating. A while back, our conversations with Johnny became more detailed. He knew Bella's name and began asking what my name was, where was my house, did Bella have a sister (Johnny proudly informed me he has a sister and she is a girl!) typical questions for a 4-year-old. I became Bella's Mom since my name can be difficult for a 4-year old's tongue.

Last night on our walk, in true form, Johnny was in his front yard, 'sploring. That is usually what he says when I ask what he is doing. 'Sploring involves some form of being on your hands and knees looking at stuff. Johnny's 'sploring has uncovered bees who are making the flowers happy, and a note his sister wrote on the sidewalk to make the walking people smile.

Back to last night. There was Johnny. But this time, his dad was with him instead of his mom. I greeted them both by saying, "Hi Johnny!" He responded with his normal "Hey Bella's Mom." His dad seemed a bit surprised that I knew his name or maybe it was because Johnny clearly knew who I was, even if it was a status defined by Bella's importance in his life. We had our customary, "What are you doing?" conversation and he told me about his quest for "lighting bugs." After a few moments, his dad seemed to be very curious about our relationship and asked, "Johnny how do you know Bella's Mom?" (or something to that affect, 'cause I was getting a little testy).

In the clearest, most confident voice, Johnny responded: "She knows my name. She talks to me every day. She's my friend."

Proverbs 18:24 (KJV), "A man who has friends must himself be friendly."

Would love to share a picture of Johnny, but I am respecting our friendship and his age.

…Go call a friend.

# The Power of Silence

Most people are not comfortable with silence.

We get in our cars and immediately connect to something: talk radio, music, something on satellite radio. The options are many. Who drives along in a quiet car?

We walk in our homes and immediately turn on something. That something is usually the television because listening to the radio at home is almost a lost art. For the high-tech folks, it may be listening to Alexa or Google. Customized messaging.

Others have perfected avoiding silence by having customized playlists. It may not be 24-hour news feeds or the latest reality show, but it is our favorite playlist that is designed to get us out of a mood or in a mood. But it is not silence.

There are some people, the ones I know will remain nameless, who avoid silence so much that they sleep with some kind of device on, again usually the television.

A recent experience left me without cable and internet service for a while. My initial reaction of *what will I do until they get this fixed* was a bit stressful. I quickly reasoned with myself that life had to be more than cable services and Wi-Fi. What about all those books that have gotten (and continue to be) delivered to your house?

"Getting Things Done." Great book by David Allen on the art of stress-free productivity.

"I no longer multi-task. I chose to focus on the tasks and activities that add the most value to my life. In doing so, whatever I am doing at the precise moment, whether personal or professional, it deserves my undivided attention." ~ J. Katrinda McQueen

# Hurt People, Hurt People

"You hurt me" is not an easy statement to make. For some reason, we prefer to walk around and suffer in silence rather than utter these three words. If we are a bit bold, we will tell our bestie, our girls, or those who will commiserate with us. Misery loves company. I will tell the ones who will support me in my hurt easier than I will tell the person who hurt me.

An interesting component of the dialogue on hurt is this basic fact: Only people we care about are truly able to hurt us. Sure, the person in the doctors' office who speaks harshly to me hurt my feelings... but the hurt only lasted until I got out of the office and back in my car. I was soon on to the next thing, not letting that hurt –that sting— linger. In the normal to and from of life in the 21$^{st}$ century, there are lots of hurts and stings every day because we seem to have lost many of the basic courtesies that have long been part of our cultural norms. We experience these and move on in rapid fashion. But, when the hurt comes from someone we love and care about, it lingers, it lasts, and it is not easily forgotten.

Why? First, we have this idea in our heads that loving and caring means never being hurt or never causing pain. If you love me and care for me, you will not hurt me. If you love me and care for me, you will be diligent in tending to all of the things that matter to me in such a way that I will never be hurt by you. Your love and care for me means that you will never forget my birthday, and you will always know what I want and what I need even without me telling you.

Sorry, it does not work that way. Why? Because we are all human. Being human means we get busy and forget birthdays. Being human means we get distracted by things at work and sometimes neglect seeking to understand what you need. Being human means that we get frustrated after repeated efforts to ask you what you want… only to hear, "you should know."

At the same time that we make assumptions about never being hurt… we also assume you know that the hurt exists. Regardless of why the hurt took place, it is more important that the hurtee and the hurter both address the issue. The person who feels hurt is responsible for saying so and the person who caused the hurt is responsible for healing the hurt.

How do we heal hurts? Not by pretending that they do not exist. It is simply by acknowledging that the hurt exists, extending sincere apologies, and working through action and reaction to reduce the chances there will be another hurt. There will be more hurts, because we are human, but at least let's try not to repeat the same hurts over and over again. Heal your own hurt so you can focus on healing those hurts that you cause to others.

# Big Girl Panties

I do words for a living. Recently, I have been spending as much time with phrases as I do with words. It is interesting (at least to me) to understand the origin of certain phrases and why they remain popular.

There are a lot of things going on in my life right now, good and bad. Feels like there is more bad than good, but I am trying hard not to keep score. Before you reach out and tell me that my life is really good and my bad is minor, let me just say, you can't define good or bad for me. Thanks for trying.

More important than what is happening is how I respond to it. I cannot control much of what happens, especially what other people do or do not do. Trying to understand why people do some of the things they do is a lot like trying to count raindrops. It is futile at best and certainly with little benefit. Since I cannot change what is happening, I can change the way I respond.

That's where "big girl panties" come in. Among women, it has become a common response to drama and issues. When seeking support for those things we cannot control or change, the response from those who really love and care for me is often, "Put your big girl panties on and get over it." The Urban Dictionary defines it as an expression that is used to say, "grow up, move on, and be an adult," (Urbandictionary.com). Others use this phrase as a sarcastic remark to a person who seems to be acting childish and immature and wallowing in self-pity. Not a good reaction no matter what is going on.

Stuff happens. People hurt us, people disappoint us, people use us. And, despite how it feels in the midst, a lot of times, what is going on has nothing to do with us. 'Makes me think of the term, "collateral damage." We are hurt by others who are going through their own set of stuff and our being hurt is just collateral damage. Maybe God will talk to me about that tomorrow.

But today, I am working on those things that are making my heart heavy and all the things that are causing me concern. As I think about Ephesians 6:13-18, the Scripture that teaches us to put on the whole armor of God, I will take the liberty of personalizing it for me. So, along with the belt of truth, the breastplate of righteousness, shoes for readiness, and the helmet of salvation, I am putting on my big girl panties and heading out to take on all that is before me.

I'm growing up, moving on, and being an adult, about EVERYTHING in my life. I will because I can.

Ephesians 6:13-18 (MSG)

"Be prepared. You're up against far more than you can handle on your own. Take all the help you can get, every weapon God has issued, so that when it is all over but the shouting you will still be on your feet. Truth, righteousness, peace, faith, and salvation are more than words. Learn how to apply them. You will need them throughout your life. God's Word is an indispensable weapon. In the same way, prayer is essential in this ongoing warfare. Pray hard and long. Pray for your brothers and sisters. Keep your eyes open. Keep each other's spirits up so that no one falls behind or drops out."

# Adjusting My Crown

Every girl should have a crown. Every woman should have a crown. In the natural evolution of life, we should progress from princess to queen. This determination does not have to come from Ancestry.com; we can simply consider it so.

There is nothing that tells a little girl she cannot be a princess. Long before there were store-bought costumes, you got some sheer curtains, aluminum foil, and cardboard, and in my very best French voice, voilà "You are a princess." Daddies routinely told their little girls, "You are my princess." There was no researching ancestry, just making it so.

Somewhere between pink and purple and royal wands, not enough princesses are becoming queens. Rather than walking and practicing our royal waves, head held high and eyes bright and smiling, we are now stooped over with the burdens of life and praying that the next "wave" is not the one that takes us out. Heads are bowed, either from exhaustion or in prayer. Eyes are tired and cold. Not feeling so royal.

Our daddies still love us and want the best for us, so what dethroned us? In most cases, we dethroned ourselves. We make daily choices and too many times we let the choices define us instead of taking control. Royalty is royalty. Once a princess, always a princess. We have to choose to live in our royalty. After all, we are eternal heirs to the throne.

Romans 8:17 (NIV) "Now if we are children, then we are heirs--heirs of God and co-heirs with Christ, if indeed we share in his sufferings in order that we may also share in his glory."

How do we get back on the throne? We simply place ourselves there. We place ourselves above all that tries to get in the way. Commit to hold your head high, defying those things that would have you bent over and stooped. You will not be pretending that they do not exist, just not letting them take complete control. Bright eyes. Yes, bright with hope. Hope and determination that things will get better. Royal wave. Yep, got it down pat–waving away all the trivial things that have gotten in the way, so many times before.

I am a planner. Today, I have added several events to the schedule, one being to adjust my crown. Your crown will not stay on if your head is bent over. Your crown will not sit well if you are waving your arms wildly about. Your crown shines brighter when your eyes are brighter. Once royalty, always royalty. If you do not have a crown, go buy one.

"Happiness is when what you think, what you say and what you do are in harmony." —*Gandhi*

# Memories...

The word has a variety of meanings in all our lives. There are a lot of songs about memories – making them and having them. Barbra Streisand sang "The Way We Were," one of the classics. While she does not technically fit the "Old School" moniker, she is indeed a classic. As one of my adopted children always tells me, you can tell if a song is really good by the number of people who remake it. So, whether you listen to Barbra, Lionel, Beyoncé, or the quintessential Gladys, give these words and their meaning the respect they deserve.

Without memories, we live in a vapor. Even the memories as close as yesterday serve a purpose in our lives. Memories of last week, last month, or even last year also have their purposes, if we allow them. Memories either fuel us or fell us. Some of the memories we hold dearest are the most painful things we own. We hold them—not to relish the pain, but more often to celebrate the lives and loves that made the memories possible. You know the saying, it is better to have loved and lost, than to have never loved at all. This could be debated by some, but even the debate is likely to be grounded in memories. After all, memories that mean something have love and loss at the core of them. Please take note… not all memories are painful.

Memories are what we make of them. Memories are pictures in our heads and hearts. We get to add the meaning to these pictures, and if we are really good, just the thought of a memory we can invoke the feelings that go along with the picture and images in our heads and hearts: Joy, hope, laughter, life, love... and yes, some hurt, pain, suffering, tears, and loss.

# Time Check

Many of us live our lives according to time. Time can be anything from the time of day, the day of the week, the week of the month, the month of the year, the actual year itself, to the decade (as in the '20's). Additional markers of time are the holidays and annual events that are marked on every standard calendar. Some are obvious, like Thanksgiving and Christmas… as if we could ever forget. Others a bit more subtle, like Flag Day or National Ice Cream Day.

Whether intentional or not, making note of the time tends to evoke certain emotions and reactions from us. If it is Veteran's Day, we think of all those who have served and for many, that is a memory of grief, not celebration. Likewise, when it is National Grandparent's Day… again, a time that should be joyous (grandchildren are better than children, you just have to endure the children to get them!)–but, for some grandparents, the day is a reminder of broken families and estrangement. Despite what the commercial landscape looks like and tries to entice us with, let's begin using these "events" as the catalyst for a time check.

Check in on someone who may not be able to put the "Happy" in front of the occasion. Check in on someone we just have not connected with in a while.

Check in on those we think are strong and have it all together.

Check in on those we know are weak and need lifting up.

"But you must not forget this one thing, dear friends: A day is like a thousand years to the Lord, and a thousand years is like a day." (1 Peter 3:8 NLT)

"But do not overlook this one fact, beloved, that with the Lord one day is as a thousand years, and a thousand years as one day." (1 Peter 3:8 ESV)

# Honoring Fathers

On July 5, 1908, a West Virginia church sponsored the nation's first event for the sole purpose of honoring fathers, a Sunday sermon in memory of the 362 men who had died in the previous December's explosions at the Fairmont Coal Company mines in Monongah, but it was a one-time commemoration and not an annual holiday (Almanac.com).[10]

Doing some work to understand why and how we have come to celebrate fathers on the 3rd Sunday of June, each year, I was touched to see that one of the very first events was rooted in the church. That is, it is rooted in the foundation that teaches us the best examples of fatherhood.

There are a couple of establishing statements that must be made. First, there is only ONE perfect Father, our God. While many of us think our earthly fathers are perfect, it is in fact, their imperfections that make them good for us. Second, I was touched by the fact that the first event was triggered by the loss of 362 men. Why are we continuing to wait for the loss of a father or father figure to recognize them and honor them?

My dad passed away in 2014. I have had more conversations with him in the years since his death than I did in the several decades we shared together. He has heard how much I love him and appreciate him in the spiritual realm, far more times than I told him in person. I have asked his advice and guidance so many more times than I can ever recall. Advice and guidance about everything that is going on in my life. I bought my first car without consulting him. I am certain he would have advised against buying a car with a manual transmission… simply because I did not know how to drive one. Now, I talk to him often about my cars, servicing them and other concerns. It is important to note here, that my dad was not a car person. He kept his cars serviced and cleaned, but was not real comfortable under a hood. Just because a person is not hands on, does not mean they cannot give you guidance and advise. I talk to him about my career, my work, my dreams, my desires, and my hopes, all in the spirit realm, simply because I did not take time to recognize the gift and blessing that would have come from having these conversations in person.

Working through these thoughts, today I thank all the fathers and father figures in my life. Thank you, Mel Porter, for being a great father and allowing me to parent with you; thank you Roosevelt Cleveland, Sr. for being a father-figure in my life for so many years, thank you Shun Reynolds, Trey Porter, Robert Porter for allowing me to see, first-hand, how great sons become great fathers. Thank you for loving your children the way you do.

My father only had daughters. For me, this means none of us were able to pass on the McQueen name to our children. I was the stubborn one who opted not to change my name when I got married. (I have since learned how disrespectful this was to my husband, and I am grateful he has forgiven me.)

As I learn the meaning and pride that comes with a name, I am grateful to Daryl McQueen and Brandon McQueen for continuing the name.

Today, I am celebrating all of the fathers who are continuing the lineage and the tradition of fathers… not perfect fathers, but perfect for the children God has gifted to them.

# Playlists

In a conversation with a talented group of ladies yesterday, the topic of modern technology came up. As we discussed the access technology provides to news, communications via text, email, photos of the grandbabies and the dog, shopping, shopping, and more shopping... the subject of music also came up. Thanks to modern technology, you no longer have to carry around individual recordings of your favorite music. Have a mobile device? Magic happens... you now have access to 57+ million songs. 1+ million playlists... through Google Play's new service, Playlist (not a commercial or an endorsement, just the facts).

Thanks to this ease of access, the current and future generations will not experience the joys of riding along, listening to the radio and being able to proudly proclaim, "That's my jam!" You sang every word and hoped somehow that the DJ knew it was your jam and would play it again, within the hour. If, and I mean IF, you were lucky, you had access to it at home via 8-track, cassette, album, or CD. Ok, enough ancient history. The message in all this seems to be that we are all moved by different things. Your playlist may not have any of the songs on my playlist, even if we are besties. The young folks may have the same songs on their playlist that I do, but I assure you they are not the same versions by the same artists. "Before I Let You Go" can be Frankie Beverly and Maze or Beyonce. The added novelty of this is that music is also described as a universal language, one that we can all understand, regardless of our native tongue. What touches us individually also touches us collectively. There would not be 57+million songs if there was not an audience for each one. There is no right or wrong playlist; it is whatever works for you.

A new idea. Is your playlist just music? What else is playing in your ears? Just like we have separate playlists for our inspirational music and our pump-up music, we also have other playlists. These activities can serve as the playbook for our lives and our days. Could the to-do list be the "playlist" for the day?

# Setting the Table

Growing up in our household involved a pretty detailed chore list. My dad was in the military, so schedules and regimens were a normal part of our daily lives. We probably should have kept it simple and just called it a duty roster, and yes, we were drafted–we did not enlist!

One of the items on the chore list was to set the table for meals. There was someone (not my mom) designated to cook the meal and the other person had to set the table and clear it after. (I was part of a two-man troop for a really long time because there is 6 years between me and the next recruit, I mean sister).

Setting the table in our house meant there was a clean tablecloth on the table, placemats, plates, napkins – properly folded— a knife, a fork, and a spoon… regardless of what was being served. Glasses with ice in them accompanied serving spoons in the middle of the table. You also placed the salt and pepper on the table, strategically near my dad's seat. This was done for every meal, every day, seating for six.

Little did I know, I was learning to create an atmosphere of expectation. With the table set, we expected a meal. On the days my mom cooked, we expected a great meal. (If you have not had a meal prepared by my mom, you have not lived!) We expected to be fed and get full. We expected conversation as my dad would always expect us to be able to talk about current events. (That table is where I learned to have an opinion.) I expected to laugh and hear stories from my parents and sisters, and I did. I expected to be heard, and I was.

Set the table in your life. Create expectations, for yourself first and then for others. Whether dining alone or with others, set the table. Set expectations for yourself and for everyone and anyone that you allow to occupy a space in your life. Prepare the table for them. Flowers make a great centerpiece. Candles and music can be everyday essentials (you may not live to see that next "special occasion"). A tablecloth is a must. Do not eat off a naked table. Use your best china (in the real and literal senses), put out all the silverware, regardless of what is being served, and use cloth napkins. Create expectations. Set the table for good food (home cooked or store bought). Water glass nice, wine glass essential, dessert plates a must!

Expect to hear and be heard. Laughter and love are always on the menu. Best served at least twice a day.

# Going Through, To Get To

I love water. My last two homes have had a body of water behind them, intended to keep me close to something that I enjoy and that brings me peace. At least, that was the plan.

At the old house, the houses were spaced such that you could not easily go around the entire lake, so there was very little human traffic in my yard. Critters of every kind… but few humans. At the current house, different story. It is still hard to go around the entire lake… but since my house is close to the walking trail, it appears now that my yard is the "cut-through." Recently this has meant I look up at various times to see children walking through my backyard. Even when I do not see them, Bella's radar knows they are out there and immediately lets me know.

A recent conversation with one of them went something like this. "May I ask why you are walking through my yard?" "I am going through to get to…" not sure what the rest of the response was. I was taken by the simplicity of the phrase… going through to get to.

Life lesson. God brought this to mind this morning. I have come to accept that this just might be the real meaning of life. Everything we do is part of going through… to get to. What challenges us most often is the not knowing what we will have to go through nor where the "to" actually is. Let me explain.

We willingly (most times) go through traffic to get to where we want to go. We willingly wait in long lines at our favorite restaurant to get the meal we want. We willingly go through nine months of weight gain, swollen feet, and sleepless nights to get to the children who are our pride and joy. It is simplified, but in these instances, we know what the "to" is going to be. And it is something we want and have made the choice to go after.

Not so willingly, we go through pain and distress when we learn we have a terminal illness. When the treatment plan is laid out, we know there is a path and that we will have to go through some things; we just do not know what the "to" will be. We go through heartache and grief when we lose a loved one. Each day is a new set of "through" and we do not know what the 'to' will ever be and have little doubt it will ever come. Pains, losses, disappointments… these are the hardest kinds of throughs.

But if we can just focus on the "other side" of through—I do not know where that is for you… for me, I just know that when I get "to" the other side, I have learned to look back. We sing a song in the Baptist church, "How I Got Over." Life does not allow us many shortcuts. We cannot cut through someone's backyard on a regular basis to get to where we need to be. Life is best lived when we go the long way… the tough lesson way… "the how in the #$@!" way.

Regardless of where you are headed or how tough it gets – do not stop. Why? It's the journey, not the destination.

"Learn the art of patience. Apply discipline to your thoughts when they become anxious over the outcome of a goal. Impatience breeds anxiety, fear, discouragement, and failure. Patience creates confidence, decisiveness, and a rational outlook, which eventually leads to success." Brian Adams, author.

#itsbaseballyall

## Very Personal

I love baseball. I am a girl who loves baseball. I am a girl with no brothers who loves baseball. I am a girl with NO athletic skills who loves baseball.

Baseball is a bat-and-ball game played between two opposing teams who take turns batting and fielding. The game proceeds when a player on the fielding team, called the pitcher, throws a ball which a player on the batting team tries to hit with a bat. (Wikipedia, 2020)[11] Simple, right?

References to games resembling baseball in the United States date back to the 18th century. Its most direct ancestors appear to be two English games: rounders (a children's game brought to New England by the earliest colonists) and cricket.

# Hearing Things

There are noises around us every day–all kinds, from many different sources. My challenge for you this day is to turn off the TV and the mobile devices and just sit and listen. Listen to really hear.

When did the refrigerator get to be so loud? Where is that car going at this time of the morning? Oh, there is the air freshener. The air conditioner just cycled on. Bella is snoring—all of this was heard in a span of less than five minutes.

So many times, we think of hearing things as a bad thing. People who hear things need professional help, or so I thought. At a pivotal time in my life when I needed to make some of the hardest decisions I have ever made, I realized there was no one who could tell me what was best for me, or what I needed to do. At least, no physical person in this realm could. Everyone has an opinion of what is best for you, and it always seems to be the opposite of what they are doing for themselves. The one person who knows what is best for me is the one person I have not been consistent in listening to.

It is not for the lack of speaking. He speaks to us every day, in many different ways. But are we hearing? Are you listening? Are you hearing things? If not, I encourage you to start today. Just like we know the sound of the devices in our homes, the sound of our cars in the driveway, or the intro music of our favorite TV program, we have to know the sound of the ones we trust. We have to hear things.

How do we learn to hear things? Find that space where you can be talked to—where things can be shared with you. For me, it's mornings. I do not turn on the TV, the radio, music, or anything else. I sit and listen. This is a crucial step; you have to be listening to hear. Also, you have to be open to what you are hearing. Block out the man-made noises like the hum of the air conditioner, or the whirring of the lawn sprinkler. Focus on hearing the things that really matter. Your thoughts, your heartbeat... what are you hearing? What are they saying... are they talking to you or others?

Start with five minutes of silence every morning. Sit quietly, not to run things through your mind, but to create an atmosphere where you can listen, and you can be spoken to, where you can hear.

Hearing things can be the best part of your life. Are you listening?

# What Do You Mean?

I love words. I love the meaning of words. Definitions are powerful. One of the words I really like is oxymoron. I like the word and the meaning is a story in itself.

An **oxymoron** is a rhetorical device that uses an ostensible self-contradiction to illustrate a rhetorical point or to reveal a paradox (Wikipedia.org).[12] A more general meaning is "contradiction in terms." In case you were wondering, the plural is **oxymorons**, and in some rare cases this is presented as **oxymora.**

Lately, the phrase "new normal" has become immensely popular. It is a bit oxymoronic, that is, a contradiction in terms. Normal is used to describe individual behavior that conforms to the most common behavior in society. New refers to something that would never have been done before. New normal suggests a new common behavior. I think that is where the rhetoric comes in.

If it is new, it will take a while for it to become normal. Do you ever wonder who is actually on the committee to make the decision that something is normal? When did it become normal for an 8-year-old (with no job or income) to own a mobile phone that costs several hundred dollars and comes with a fairly sizeable monthly bill? Who decided it was normal for conference calls to start at 7AM and that getting calls at 7PM was part of a normal workday?

Whoever is making the decisions… I politely want to let you know that I have come to the realization that it is best for me to decide my own "normal."

Much of what I have been experiencing is not new. My new normal is a return to those things that have kept me grounded for so long, and that give my life meaning: My faith, my family, my friends and my focus.

# More Godwinks

If you have not read any of Squire Rushnell's God Winks Books... please do so!

He says, "In my definition of a Godwink, I contend that it encompasses answered prayer. A personal signal or message directly from God, sometimes as an answer to prayer, and often mislabeled as coincidence." Source: "When God Winks on New Beginnings," p. 33.

Godwinks are little things that Squire Rushnell says are the small ways that God speaks to us. Thank you, God, for this morning. A memory came up today on Facebook. It was one of the last pictures I took with my dad, and then as I was going through some papers, I found a letter my dad sent to me 12 years ago! Every Father's Day gets harder than the last ... but God winks to let me know I will be ok.

"When the voice and vision on the inside become more profound, clearer, and louder than the opinions on the outside, you have mastered your life." John DeMartini, author ... Condensed version: My voice is the only one that needs to be in my head.

# Hustle and Flow

It is bad when morning prayer leaves me thinking about rap songs. This is definitely not caused by the person leading prayer.

It is Monday morning. Mondays get a bad rap. Mornings get a bad rap almost every day.

Mondays signal the start of a new week, and for many, a new grind. Ironically enough, young people have begun using the term grind to refer to their jobs, but the term was actually coined in the 1800s. Informally, grind also means boring, tedious work, often in the sense of "grind away" or "the daily grind." This sense of grind was invented in the 1800s as college slang. And yet, while one definition makes it sound hard and demeaning, another suggests positive outcomes. In millwork, grind means sharpen, smooth, or produce (something) by crushing or by friction, as in "power from a waterwheel was used to grind cutlery" (Dictionary.com).[13]

Several years ago, there was a movie released called, "Hustle and Flow." In the movie, a pimp (Terrence Howard) in Memphis, Tennessee, sees rap music as the way to escape his dead-end existence and achieve something meaningful. The movie has some very poignant moments but stays in my mental library for one of the songs from the soundtrack, "It's Hard Out Here for a Pimp."

Before all of my friends start calling Pastor Q and telling him I need an intervention and serious prayer… stay with me. The first few lines of the song talk about how hard it can be for someone in this line of work. It is expensive.

First, you are on your own for the exact words to the song. My suggestion, play the song ONLY when you are alone and using headphones. There is spicy language throughout.

Second, I am not condoning this behavior. I am just reminding all of us that the grind is real. Everyone faces Mondays. Everyone, regardless of what business you are in, faces the start of a new work week, a new business month, a new sales cycle… something. And facing it is not always easy.

In a previous role, the lives of the whole team were driven by month-end. Month-end consumed every waking moment for at least two to three days, if we were lucky. There was a tremendous sigh of release when we got on the other side of it… but only to realize that the next month had already started and in most cases, we had 2-3 days of catch up to do to get back on track for the next month-end. Grind.

"Hustle and Flow" is a good reference for daily life. We all know we have commitments and obligations, and that as responsible adults, we do whatever it takes to meet them. That's the hustle. Jobs, careers, families, children, church, social obligations… the list goes on. At the same time, we know that the hard work pays off. As Isaiah 65 says, we live in houses we did not build; we eat food we did not grow, and we get to enjoy a multitude of blessings that we do not deserve. That's the flow.

We are indeed working to get the money for the rent, for the cars and the gas money spent… No matter how dull or how tedious, no matter the grind, we all end up in a better space when we realize that the grind sharpens, smooths, and produces something in all of us.

# The Book of Common Sense

Please turn with me in your Bibles, to the Book of Common Sense, chapter 25.

My church (it always feels good to say that... not that I own it, but that I belong to a body of believers) reads through the book of Proverbs during the month of May. It is a simple task; just read the chapter that corresponds to the date. I have done this many times. It is a great way to learn to read the Bible and to create some consistency in your daily devotion. I have read through alone and in groups. EVERY time I read the book of Proverbs, I learn something.

After the church finished, I decided to do it again. In May, I read using the Tony Evans Study Bible (should be required for every household). This time, I decided to read through Proverbs using the Message Bible. Hence, today's musing, the Book of Common Sense.

Some things are just obvious, or so I thought. For example, if you approach an intersection, you should be prepared to stop. You should not have to look for a sign to tell you that traffic traveling in two different directions can be a dangerous thing. It is dangerous even when there is a stop sign or a traffic light.

Common sense. It should be equally obvious that you should not lend money you cannot afford to lose. You honestly cannot be mad at the borrower if they do not pay you back. You are lending the money to them, and you had it to spare so… obvious. If you need your money, at any point, keep your money. Simple.

These are the kinds of things that Proverbs teach us. Yes, I said teach. The state of the modern world suggests that too many people cut class and missed lessons on common sense. It is becoming truly clear, that common, is not so common anymore. Today's reading of Proverbs included the following. You decide.

Proverbs 25:2 (MSG)

God delights in concealing things;

scientists delight in discovering things.

25:6-7

Don't work yourself into the spotlight;

don't push your way into the place of prominence.

It's better to be promoted to a place of honor

than face humiliation by being demoted.

25:8

Don't jump to conclusions—there may be

a perfectly good explanation for what you just saw.

25:9-10

In the heat of an argument,

don't betray confidences;

Word is sure to get around,

and no one will trust you.

25:12

The right word at the right time

is like a custom-made piece of jewelry,

Now, for the benediction.

# Budget Committee

I am a planner. With the introduction of PDA's (personal daily assistants also known as devices that let us set reminders and to do's using keyboards, a stylus, or voice control), it has become easy for me to plan and schedule those recurring events that need to take place in my life. Some I look forward to like Blow Money Monday, others, like today… not so much. Let me explain.

Four or five days before the month ends is always a Budget Committee meeting. It is scheduled to occur on the 26th of each month for the rest of my life (or at least as long as I own this phone). This is the day the committee meets to handle all financial matters for the upcoming month. The idea and the concept belong to Dave Ramsey, but I have my own process.

Let me start by saying, avoiding the topic of financial matters does not help. Whether we have money or not, we are all called to be good stewards over whatever we have been entrusted with. Even if that is a stack of bills that you cannot pay, there is still a responsibility to know who you owe and what you owe them. (You just might be missing out on an opportunity. Another story for another day.) In scope for the Budget Committee at my house are all the items that are on the balance sheet, and all of the items that contribute to net worth. That means the budget committee is responsible for all bank accounts (regardless of the balance), the house, the cars, the clothes, the vacation account,

Blow Money Monday… all of it. (Blow Money Monday is the one Monday a month that you can spend (blow) money without consulting the budget committee.)

Second, it is also important to understand that "it is not what you have, it's what you choose to do with it." You can choose to use your house payment for a vacation as long as you are ok with being worried about how to make it up. It used to be called robbing Peter to pay Paul. You can choose to make bad choices as long as you are willing to accept the consequences of those choices. Every choice has a consequence. The committee vote stands.

And then… your budget committee is only responsible for you and yours. Not the Jones, not the Smiths… nor those people you do not know but feel you need to impress. Just you and yours.

My budget committee process is simple. I start with prayer. Some sources say there are well over 2,000 verses in the Bible about money. I start in prayer simply because I have a well-documented track record that says I can't do this by myself. Proverbs 3:6 (NIV) says, "In all thy ways acknowledge him, and he shall direct thy paths." After wandering for far too many years, I have learned that my financial path is one of those "ways" in which I needed to acknowledge Him. And, when I did. Oh my. Let me simply say, Ephesians 3:20 is true. (I will wait while you look it up.)

Over the years, I have learned to keep it simple, and now, I must admit, that I do not dread the appointment. It took a few simple steps to get me here. Before I head off to meet with the committee, here are a few things I learned along the way:

1. ALWAYS start and END in prayer

2. Avoiding the issue does not make it go away

3. Write it down, make it happen

4. Regarding debt: the borrower is servant to the lender. Just do not borrow.

5. Stuff: the less you have, the less you have to manage

6. Small matters: saving $5 dollars at a time still adds up

7. It is only a deal if you were willing to pay full price AND put the difference between full price and the bargain in your savings account. Otherwise… you really did not save that 70%

8. Having positive bank balances is like doing math with a 4-year-old: she feels she can add as many zeroes as she wants to her numbers.

9. Assets are NOT things you wear on your body or drive; they are the gifts entrusted to you to bless others!

10. You cannot beat God in giving, no matter how you try!

Committee adjourned.

# Quarters, Dimes, Nickels, and Pennies

On the fiscal calendar, June 30th is the end of the quarter. A quarter is simply three months. So, June is the end of the three-month period that started April 1st. Many businesses evaluate their progress against their annual goals on a quarterly basis. According to finance-zacks.com, "when a company reports quarterly earnings, it is giving a glimpse into its financial performance from the most recent three-month period. Investors often use these results to determine whether to buy or sell a stock."

The next several days will be terribly busy for CPAs and others in the financial industry, and especially so this year as all companies are working to navigate and mitigate the effects of the pandemic. Last week, when the McQueen Budget Committee met, we considered the second quarter and made some startling discoveries.

It all matters: Pennies, nickels, dimes, and quarters. Not from a financial perspective always, but in general. Do you remember the first time you saw a penny on the ground? You were probably a child and thought, "Wow," I found some money. Then as we got older, we morphed into thinking, why would I bother to stop and pick up a penny? Have you considered that pennies are those trivial things in life that add up to be meaningful? One hundred pennies are still a dollar. If you saw the one-dollar bill on the ground, you would strongly consider picking it up, right? There are 365 days in the year. Don't miss the pennies around you every day... they add up.

Nickels are kinda' like weeks. A nickel is worth five cents. If we are technical about it, we can say the week has five days and then we get a weekend. For most of us, getting through the five days of the work week is an ongoing accomplishment. Our nickels. Make those five workdays the most productive you can. Give more than you get. Leave the workday knowing, with confidence, that you have given your best. If you are lucky, you learned something AND you taught something to someone else. Nickels on the ground make us think a little harder at picking them up... but have you noticed, you rarely see nickels on the ground. There are 52 weeks in the year. Twenty nickels make that one dollar. That number is fewer than the number of pennies it takes, but they still add up.

Dimes. Not the Charlie Wilson (American singer and musician) kind. Dimes are like our months. Compressed, they are smaller than pennies and nickels, but worth more. Once you get through an entire month you realize how much time has passed. Days do turn into weeks and weeks do turn into months, whether we want them to or not. The planning process that I created for myself involves making daily goals, weekly goals, and monthly goals These are not radical things, just interests, desires, and needs. Yes, each month still has a goal to research options for the next vacation... even though I have no idea when I will get to go anywhere. Let's just say, I will be sitting on ready when the time comes. There are topics to research, projects to do in the house, and things that take incremental steps to accomplish.

That is why they are monthly. I need a few more days to work on them than the hours I get in a week. There are 12 months in the year, Dimes have collective value just like the others… ten dimes make a dollar. They are smaller, it takes fewer, but in the end they have the same value.

Quarters. In mathematics, a quarter is one fourth. Quarters are what started this conversation. The second quarter has ended so another fourth of the year is gone. Another three months. Quick… what have you accomplished in the last three months? Remember what we started with… "quarterly reports give an investor a glimpse of the financial performance of a company so they can determine if they want to buy into the company or sell what they already have in the company." You have given up three months of the year. Are you pleased with what you have to show for it? Would you invest in you for another three months? Are there things in your life you need to sell off? Are there things that are contributing to poor performance? Regardless of who you are and what you do, you owe it to yourself to be the best you possible. And guess what? You get to set the standard. You are Me, Inc.

An interesting side note: I love books and was amazed to learn there is a book called "Me, Inc." written by Gene Simmons. Yes, mascara-wearing, KISS, Gene Simmons. It would make for great reading on this topic. Here is what made me read it:

The fact that KISS is one of the most successful rock bands in the world is no accident. "From the beginning Gene Simmons and Paul Stanley had a clear-cut vision of what they wanted to do and how they wanted to operate KISS *as a business* well before they ever first took the stage. Since deciding with Paul to manage the band themselves, Simmons has proved himself to be a formidable businessman, having sold over 100 million CDs and DVDs worldwide, overseen over 3,000 licensed merchandise items, and starred in the longest running celebrity reality show to date. More impressive is that he handles all of his business ventures on his own—no personal assistant, few handlers, and as little red tape as possible" (Goodreads.com).[14]

Looking back is a fantastic way to look forward.

# Priorities

The longer you live, the older you get, the more things change; what is important and what you focus on changes, as well.

Observe a two-year-old. The priority seems to be to take the toy that the other child has. Nothing more, nothing less. It is amazing that they are able to block out any other toy in the room and I assure you there are plenty. What is important is to take the one the other child has. Why... maybe just to prove they can, or to at least to create enough ruckus that some adult will step in and take the toy from both of them.

Fast forward along the age spectrum and the priority becomes fitting in and being accepted. There is concern with height. Am I taller than most kids in my grade... or shorter? Both are seen as bad. Do I have friends? Am I painfully shy? My focus becomes my priority... whatever that is.

The teenage years are ruthless. There are so many priorities that almost nothing is accomplished. Boys. Hair. Clothes. Friends. Nails. Sports. Dates. How can you ever tell what the number one priority is?

College settles some of these challenges but also brings a new set of priorities. Career choices. What sorority? What fraternity? Marriage prospects?

# Down In the Valley

Thanks to urbanization, the country has changed. Replacing rolling hills and green pastures are acres and acres of concrete—buildings, highways, streets, and roads. All designed to accommodate the vision of modern man and seemingly to obliterate the vision of the One who created them in the first place. (Different conversation for a different day.)

The presence of the urbanized landscape means that many people do not recall seeing hills and valleys. Trust me, if you grew up in the concrete jungles of most major cities, there might have been a few hills but not many valleys.

Valleys are low places. From an agricultural perspective, "a valley is a low area of land between hills or mountains, typically with a river or stream flowing through it. From an architectural perspective, a valley is an internal angle formed by the intersecting planes of a roof, or by the slope of a roof and a wall." (Dictionary.com).[15] Both definitions can readily apply to the emotional or psychological construct of being in a valley.

When people get into a valley, they often feel like they are in a low place. It feels like being surrounded by mountains–big, huge, unscalable mountains. In the valley, the stream does not evoke memories of a lazy winding stream, but more of a rolling river and the feeling of being washed away, if you are not careful—being swept up by the current. If your valley is not a rural one, the intersecting angles of the roof and the wall are equally telling.

Kinda' like being between a rock and a hard place. What seems to be most troubling about being in a valley is finding a way out. Knowing that you are in a low place creates some desire to move to higher ground, but... how do you get there? Unfortunately, it means having to climb your way out, one step, and one pull at a time. And yes, as with most climbing activities, there will be times when you slide back down, losing all the forward momentum that you worked so hard to create. But keep climbing. Climbing builds strength, and strength fuels courage, and courage creates confidence.

Oh, Lord, I'm striving trying to make it through this barren land,

As I go from day to day, I can hear my Savior say, "Trust me child, I'll hold your hand."

# Last Day

Today is the last day of the month. If you are a planner, like me, you manage things in increments like hours, days, weeks, months, quarters, and years. The whole goal with this planning stuff is to not be overwhelmed by the myriad of things that we have to (and want to) accomplish. If we somehow manage to write them down and space them out, we just might be able to get them all done.

In addition to the increments of hours, days, weeks, months, quarters, and years, sequence and position have become equally important. It is really kind of simple. If it is the first day of the week... I have six more chances to get things done. If it is the first week of the month... it feels like I have three more pretty broad windows and I have a high confidence level. The first month of the year, I feel like Goliath with 11 months ahead; I can surely conquer the world. With quarters, even though the numbers are small, the first quarter suggests a long ramp ahead. With years... let's just say, my last birthday was viewed very differently than my 25th birthday.

Ok, we just covered sequence, so let's add position. With position, only two positions really matter... first and last. When it is the first position, there is a lot of optimism...lots of ideas and thoughts about what we need to do, what we want to do, thoughts and ideas about things to explore... almost an open slate, just waiting to be filled. Excitement exists about what can be, and what might be. But, oh… if it is the last day, the emotions and the feelings can be vastly different.

On the last day, we can either be reflective and proud, or anxious. Being reflective comes from looking back at all that we were able to accomplish. We can be proud of the days where we stuck to plan, got things done, and checked things off. Anxiety comes when we look at the things that remain… some things not started at all, some things started and in various stages of undone… some things just plain forgotten about, and even some that were deliberately ignored. It is the last day of the… fill in the blank. I can lament over the "status of things," or I can be encouraged by what I call the Power of One. In my Mastermind Group, we support each other by affirming that one still has power. If I have started one thing… I am at least ahead. When we talk about 3-D View (another Mastermind concept) we are encouraged again by the Power of One. We make sure we have one's in our view. Why? Because one leads to two. If I can manage one day, and it is the Lord's will, tomorrow will be "two days" that I have managed. And it becomes exponential.

Today is the last day of the month. It also happens to be the last day of the week. So, I will close out the day, close out a week, and close out a month. Whatever the closings look like… they are what they are. But the best part, the good part, the sure part…

After last comes first… and with first… comes new chances.

There is a poem "A New Day" by Heartsill Wilson that includes this wording…

"This is the beginning of a new day. God has given me this day to use as I will. I can waste it or use it for good. What I do today is important, because I am exchanging a day of my life for it. When tomorrow comes, this day will be gone forever, leaving something in its place I have traded for it. I want it to be a gain, not a loss; good, not evil; success, not failure — in order that I shall not forget the price I paid for it." Heartsill Wilson, poet.

# Keep Standing

Over the past several days there have been many public references to James 1:4 which tells us, "Let perseverance finish its work so that you may be mature and complete, not lacking anything." It is being used as a message of encouragement.

As a noun, perseverance is defined as doing something despite difficulty, or delay in achieving success. Why is the occasion or situation related to this effort attached to difficulty or delay? Why are we not called to persevere when we are on the defined road to success, clearly able to see our destination in view?

What we are trying to do is often represented by the level of effort required to get it done... or in the rewards attached to the completion of the effort. Losing weight is an easy example of this. The level of effort to lose weight (at least for most of us) is the first of the struggles associated with reaching our desired weight goal. Then comes the sacrifice of avoiding those things that present themselves as enjoyment only to become pounds that easily and readily attach to our hips. The level of effort, the sacrifices, the time, the focus, the attention... perseverance. It is hard to continue the diet despite difficulty AND delays in achieving success. If we are lucky, one day, we happen to get on the scale and "miracles" have taken place. Ounces have been lost. Is this perhaps perseverance finishing its work? Maybe... in its simplest form.

Perseverance in its most tangible form is life—doing things that often give the appearance of being on a treadmill—moving at a steady pace, going nowhere. You might be putting in the effort, sweating and laboring for breath, yet struggling to reach the desired destination. Difficulty is a fact of life. In fact, many of our elders are quick to say, if your life has not had any difficulty, you are likely only days old–a newborn.

If not difficulty, there is often delay. Most lives, when we are honest, are filled with dreams and desires. Simple things at first… like walking and talking, and then a bit more complex like when we learn to ride a bike and then learning to drive. Dreams and desires about careers and jobs, families and children—the list is extensive and varied. Yet, in these same lives, the achievement of these dreams and goals is not only difficult, but often delayed. For some, delay means coming much later than our efforts warrant. For others, delay means not coming at all. Yet, we have no way to tell that the delay is eminent. It is only after we have put in the effort, and done the work, that we realize the difficulties and the delays. What then?

Keep standing. To get the strength, stamina, motivation, and energy to keep standing, and to persevere, we have to back up to the beginning of the first chapter of James. James 1:2-4 (NIV) gives us a clearer perspective: "Consider it pure joy, my brothers and sisters, whenever you face trials of many kinds, because you know that the testing of your faith produces perseverance. Let perseverance finish its work so that you may be mature and complete, not lacking anything". Keep standing, stand with a smile, stand with courage and determination, and stand with faith. The test guarantees the outcome. The testing of our faith assures us that we will be able to keep doing something despite difficulty, or delay in achieving success. The testing of our faith assures us that we can persevere.

Keep standing. Standing on the promises of Christ our Savior, standing on the promise that perseverance will finish its work, we will not lack anything.

# Planting Trees

I have had to make a lot of decisions lately, some that included trees. In fact, the tree decisions have been some of the hardest. The landscape architect shows you pictures of beautiful trees that he thinks will look great in your yard. You then stand out in front of your house and try to imagine those trees… the ones in the pictures… in your yard. Even worse, you go to the nursery, only to realize that in order to have the image in the pictures you have to spend a small fortune. The trees in the pictures were 8-10 feet tall, and that height comes with a price. Of course, you can purchase the 2-4 feet ones for a more reasonable price and wait (and trust) that they will grow to look like the larger ones. Choices. Options.

That (with all the other decisions I am in the midst of) made me realize that perhaps the first thing I need to plant is a decision tree. I used to use them at work a lot. Not sure why I got away from it, other than the fact that things now seem to happen so fast that there is not much time to really analyze the decision components. You just hope for the best.

A decision tree. According to Wikipedia, "A decision tree is a decision support tool that uses a tree-like model of decisions and their possible consequences, including chance event outcomes, resource costs, and utility. It is one way to display an algorithm that only contains conditional control statements."[16] Yep, one of those should go in the center of the front yard. When making any decision, you have to consider the consequences. If I go with the mature trees, I will deplete my savings account. The consequence is that I will not be prepared for any emergency that might come after. The branches of the decision tree start to form when you consider all the variations of options. One mature tree and several small ones or two mature, fewer small ones, or of course, the realistic choice... all small ones. "No trees" is not an option according to my HOA. Well, it is, but at the cost of SEVERAL mature trees.

For the simple things like what to have for breakfast, or what to watch on TV, we consider options and make the decision in milliseconds. Deciding what to wear (for some people) can take a lot longer and involve physical options known as trying things on. But, what about those essential parts of our lives, when it comes to making decisions about those critical, life-changing matters? Those things can change the path we take, the people on the path with us, and in some cases, even the destination.

While I appreciate the science behind the model, and the way it helps me finalize the landscape plan for the decisions that really matter... this simple tune plays in my head:

"I have decided to follow Jesus, I have decided to follow Jesus, I have decided to follow Jesus. No turning back, no turning back. Though none go with me, I still will follow, though none go with me, I still will follow, Though none go with me, I still will follow... No turning back, no turning back." (Hymn attributed to Sadhu Sundar Singh).

# #Happy Running

I have a shirt that has this message on it. Every time I see it, I have mixed emotions. I have a love/hate relationship with running. Mainly I think it is a mean joke. Happy is not the word I use the majority of the time. I am a "has been." I was a runner until I made significant investments in pins and screws, in my feet and knees, as in, both of my feet and both of my knees. The warranty for all those parts said that I should be able to run again! Now I am a "wanna be" runner. You know the kind, the one with all the outfits and all the matching running shoes (custom fit, no less… thanks Phidippidies (Atlanta based running store)). I have all of the equipment… yes, running requires equipment. I have all the books, and I subscribe to all the running magazines. And… I hate running. I hate the sweating, the gasping for air, the swollen feet and knees, the aching back… and the puking that happens at certain milestones. I simply hate it. Happy? Not.

Not happy. Why? It is not running's fault. It is all mine. I want to go from zero to marathon in a week. Ok… a month? It is not happy because I do not want to do the work. I do not want to start with the basics, like starting with understanding my pace. Incremental goals… why can't I just lace up and hit the pavement? Why can't I just go out and run a nice pace that lets me best my PR and finish up glistening? Then after a nice hot bath, I'll be off to the next thing.

#Happy can be the predecessor to a whole lot of things. #HappyDieting… #HappySavingMoney… the only requisite is that what follows "Happy" has to be something that it takes time to accomplish—time, patience, discipline and dedication. All the things that tend to make us not so happy about doing it…but wait, that is the key to really being happy!

Once we are able to accept the fact that it is a journey and not a destination, we can make the appropriate adjustments and are actually able to be happy about the fact that we have made a choice and a decision… and that we are taking action. #happyrunning means I am at least on the pavement. The outfit may not match the shoes; I may be doing more walking than running, and I may just choose to alter my path and my mileage… but I am out there, and I am doing more than nothing.

#happy "anything" does not have to be a struggle. It does not have to be stressful. It is about our attitude towards it. Once the attitude changes… I promise, you will find that you approach the journey in a whole new way. One of my daily affirmations is… I choose to be happy. Maybe that is what the # should be.

I got a new attitude. Some of it is fueled by the wonderful piece that I now own that says, "Happy Everything!"

# Snakes

A very small snake was in my garage. I am terrified of snakes. Any size, any kind. This one particularly troubled me for a lot of reasons. First, it was a baby which means it has parents somewhere… are they in the garage also? Then, after looking a little more closely as it slithered away, it looked to me like a Pygmy Rattlesnake… as in a ridiculously small, but still lethal rattlesnake. What? And how, just how, did you get in MY garage?

Of course, I began to pray in earnest. After all, isn't that what we do when we are facing danger? It was one of those "get right to the point" prayers. "Lord, please do not let this snake bite me… or Bella. Oh Lord, Bella is so nosy and so low and close to the ground. How do I keep her away from danger? Lord, why me? Especially after my resident critter experts have sold their house and moved to the West Coast! After coaching me through gators and mountain lions… I am going out with a pygmy rattler AFTER they leave??"

Danger. The very thought of it causes a flight reaction in most people. All we can think of is how to get away from the danger… even if getting away will harm us more. Think about running from a black bear. If you have ever been in bear country, all of the signs and warnings tell you NOT to run, but that is all we can think of. Revelation: no matter how fast you can run a 440-yard dash, you cannot outrun a half-ton black bear. I will also acknowledge that there are people like storm chasers who go after danger, but as I do, I will go back to my first point: most of us have a flight reaction when faced with danger.

Back to the garage visitor. After managing to negotiate my life for his, I set about really trying to find out what kind of visitor he was. After all, knowledge is power, and I needed to know if I was going to have to turn over my garage to him and his family. As I was doing my research, this quote came to mind and caused me to really stop in my tracks. "Let me not pray to be sheltered from dangers, but to be fearless in facing them. Let me not beg for the stifling of my pain, but for the heart to conquer it." Rabindranath Tagore, poet.

SO very telling. As I work to be a better, stronger person, I pray to be able to live this mantra–to live a life that allows me to be fearless in facing dangers, known and unknown, and sometimes seen and unseen. Whenever, however… I want to be fearless in facing them, even in the presence of pain. Lord, give me the heart to conquer any dangers I may face, today and always.

The snake WAS a Juvenile Black Racer. May he rest in peace.


Psalm 91:4 (NLT) "He will cover you with his feathers. He will shelter you with his wings. His faithful promises are your armor and protection."

# Hidden Figures

Several years ago, there was a book (by Margot Lee Shetterly) and subsequently a movie with this title. Both tell the story of black female mathematicians who worked at the National Aeronautics and Space Administration (NASA) during the Space Race. Obviously, the Space Race and all things NASA at the time were 6:00 news so how could there be anything hidden? If you have not read the book or seen the movie… stop now and do that. None of this makes sense without knowing their story.

In every success story, there are main characters, and then there are the characters who REALLY make things happen. It reminds me of the saying, "behind every great man, there is an even greater woman." This is the story of "Hidden Figures."

I am in the midst of my own personal success story. Today, as I penned another entry in that story, I realized it is my responsibility to make sure that the wonderful people in my life who are loving me, encouraging me, and nudging me through this, are not hidden. Just like the ladies in the book and the movie, they know who they are and what they are doing. They also know how critically important their work is to me… and my success. They are not expecting to see a list of their names and what they have done (well, a few will). Rather, they want and need to see me look them in the eyes, hold their hands, and genuinely and honestly tell them thank you. They have long heard my fears and concerns, as well as my doubts and my anxieties. And each, in their own way, have responded with the words I so desperately needed to hear–not once, but over and over again.

Someone told me that I was lucky to have these people in my life. I am lucky to have found supporters and encouragers. It made me wonder… how many of us have these great supporters and encouragers in our lives, but simply do not realize it. How many of us have our own hidden figures?

Do not let them hide in plain sight. Acknowledge them, today, now.

Isaiah 45:3-5 (NIV)

"I will give you hidden treasures, riches stored in secret places, so that you may know that I am the LORD, the God of Israel, who summons you by name.

For the sake of Jacob my servant, of Israel my chosen, I summon you by name and bestow on you a title of honor, though you do not acknowledge me.

I am the LORD, and there is no other; apart from me there is no God. I will strengthen you, though you have not acknowledged me."

# Being Have

Children begin developing their vocabularies around age two. Young children are like sponges, so it is important to teach them the words you want them to know… not necessarily just the ones they hear most often in their environment (remember they do not know the difference from profanity and praise, they just know what they hear). I am not an advocate of baby talk. It is my humble opinion that using real words helps expand the vocabulary. The risk in this is teaching the words but not taking time to explain what they mean.

A situation with my dear friend's son recently reminded me of this. He is a wonderful precocious child (to those of us who do not live with him 24/7). He asks lots of questions, many that seem out of context for the four years he has been around. Sometimes I think he enjoys the asking more than he does getting an answer. In a recent situation, his mother admonished him to "behave." She warned that not behaving would likely get him in serious trouble. I had taken him a gift card so he could order some new books… since TiTi cannot take him on our regular date to Barnes and Noble. He was so excited he kept interrupting the conversation I was having with his mother and again was warned to behave. A few minutes after the second warning, I noticed he had gotten really quiet. This is generally not good for a four-year-old.

After finding him in his room, sitting on the floor, looking really sad… I asked him what he was doing. His response: "Being Have." It took every ounce of strength I had to not laugh. Fortunately, I saw it as a teaching moment and took advantage of it. All children play what I call the name game. It is when you ask, who am I while pointing to various family members. It teaches words like aunt and uncle, sister or brother, and the classic Mommy and Daddy. When we do this, we teach not just the word, but also the meaning.

Being have. What does that really mean? Being something that we are not? Being something we have no desire to be? Being something we were not designed to be?

# Gracefully Failing

Most of the goals we have in our lives are ones set by us. Even when the doctor gently suggests we should lose 10 pounds, we take that 10-pound goal… and make it 20. I will show you.

Goals, wishes, dreams… whatever you choose to call them, are future destinations. Only you will know when you have arrived. Wikipedia gives us some direction by stating: "A goal is an idea of the future or desired result that a person or a group of people envision, plan and commit to achieve. People endeavor to reach goals within a finite time by setting deadlines" (Wikipedia. com).[17]

And therein lies the challenge. Future, desired, result. Envision, plan, and commit to achieve. Where is my guarantee? Surely if I envision it, I highly desire it, and I commit to achieve it, it must be a done deal. Not so. The best laid plans, and the strongest desire ever, are not enough.

On the journey to our goals, wishes and dreams, there is this thing called life. It is full of daily ups and downs, ins and outs, and challenges and opportunities—none of which seem to care about our plans or our desires and certainly not our goals. Have I failed yet again? Along comes grace.

As you age, every day becomes more special. Everyday events take on new meanings. Having goals remains a priority, but how you respond to not meeting them changes. Or at least it has changed for me. Psalm 103:8 -12 (NIV) says, "The LORD is compassionate and gracious, slow to anger, abounding in love. He will not always accuse, nor will he harbor his anger forever; he does not treat us as our sins deserve or repay us according to our iniquities. For as high as the heavens are above the earth, so great is his love for those who fear him; as far as the east is from the west, so far has he removed our transgressions from us."

If He gives me grace, so can I. I can accept that I have fallen short, regardless of the reason. At the same time, I can be encouraged and motivated by this same grace to try again. And again. And again. I can be failing to meet the goals I set for myself. That is ok. In these situations, God knows my heart, and He is gracious and merciful, always covering my heart. I can be failing and falling, but when I am covered in grace, the landing is ever so gentle.

# Sweat the Small Stuff

"Don't sweat the small stuff" has been a popular phrase for the past decade or so. It seems to be intended to encourage people not to worry about the "little things." Over the past few weeks, as part of another set of work that I am doing, I have been laser focused on what the "petty things" are in my life. I was examining them with the goal of identifying those petty things that seem to hang me up. What a revelation! I have an extensive list of trivial things. Remember, I am a writer and a planner. I write everything down—sometimes to my lament. In an effort to get a better handle on my time, I decided to write down all the little things. For example, I noticed that I somehow lost 15 minutes between waking up and being ready to walk out the door for my morning walk. How can that be? All I do is wash face/brush teeth/put on shorts and sneakers… that cannot take 15 minutes. When I included the unimportant things… Wow! I actually:

- make the bed–even stopping to change the sheets two mornings each week!
- wash my face
- brush my teeth
- put on my shorts and sneakers
- open the blinds
- turn on the coffee pot
- check my vitals
- take first medicine

- check for critical messages on my work phone
- turn off the house alarm
- grab the leash
- then head out the door.

I also learned; I do not really sweat most of these things. So many of them are ingrained that I do them without thinking. I am an advocate of B.J. Fogg's "Tiny Habits." It is a great book if you have not read it. Tiny habits trigger bigger habits. Each little thing can lead to a bigger thing. That is when I had my AHA moment. While I am not sweating these tiny habits, I am also encouraged by one of my favorite scriptures, as I do this work. Matthew 25:23 NKJV, "His lord said to him, "Well done, good and faithful servant; you have been faithful over a few things, I will make you ruler over many things. Enter into the joy of your lord."

Rev. James Goolsby, Jr., a friend and a respected pastor, penned these words in an article for the Macon Telegraph: "Rather than focusing on more, I am going to use what I have to God's glory. I am determined to value everything that God has given me stewardship of in a way that the master will say well done thy good and faithful servant. I encourage you to value every gift that you have been given in a way that pleases our God. Whether it is your marriage, your children, your home, your job, your friends, your loved ones, your possessions, your health, or your ministry, to name a few."[18] *(Quote used with permission from James W. Goolsby Jr., who is senior pastor at First Baptist Church.)*

Some people think that being faithful over a few things is dramatically different from "sweating the small stuff". I think not. Sweating the small stuff is actually a way of making sure that we are faithful over the little things so that we can be blessed by and through the bigger, more meaningful things in our lives. Focus on those little things, those little habits, which will create memorable moments. Forgoing the laundry to make homemade ice cream. Small stuff. Homemade ice cream to share with neighbors. Value Gift.

When we pray for God to enlarge our territory, we have to remember that the landscape includes a lot of little things.

# The Corners of My Mind

One of my favorite songs has these words....

A lot of things have changed around us. Our daily routines, where we go, what we take with us when we go, who we go with... everything has changed. It is not all bad, but it sure is all different. And, when things are different, we long for the familiar—the way we were.

If we are honest with ourselves while going through these uncertain times, the way we were was not perfect; it had its challenges. There were things we were mumbling and grumbling about, but they were familiar and easy. We wanted things to be different, wanted the pace of life to slow down—we just wanted to be the ones to decide when and how, if at all.

Psalm 143:5 (MSG), "I remember to think about the many things you did in years gone by. Then I lift my hands in prayer, because my soul is a desert, thirsty for water from you."

# Dance Like No One is Watching...

I keep hitting rough patches. Really rough patches—the knock you down, almost take you out kind of rough patches. Today, I heard something that gave me some new perspective to these patches: "When you stumble, make it part of the dance." It is attributed to River Maria Urke, poet.

Music is one of the ways I get through the rough patches. I start with Scripture but sometimes need a little something that rings in my ears and kind of sticks to my ribs. It is something that most of the time, only I can hear.

Today, stumbling took me to one of my all-time favorites, Gladys Knight's version of "I Hope You Dance."

You never change your life until you step out of your comfort zone; change begins at the end of your comfort zone." ~ Roy T. Bennett, author

# Wants, Needs, and Necessaries

In a recent discussion with a few of my closest friends, we talked about the difference between wants and needs. It was interesting that we all had the same perspectives about what you "need" in life versus what you just "want." As you mature, these differences become very clear.

Maturity also introduces another component – necessaries. Needs are the basics like shelter, food, clothing—essentials. Wants, for me, are the extras. More clothes than I need, manicures, pedicures, the niceties. Necessaries are those things in life that you just have to go through, things you just have to get through.

Saving money. Necessary. Getting mammograms. Necessary. Going to the dentist. Necessary. Writing a will. Necessary. Dealing with aging parents. Necessary. Our logical mind assures us that these are things that we must do, things that must be dealt with… things that are responsible and necessary.

Every day of living offers opportunities to realize goals and dreams. Along with these ambitions are the management of wants and needs, and yes, necessaries. Jack Canfield, one of the authors of the Chicken Soup book series, reminds us:

"As you begin to take action toward the fulfillment of your goals and dreams, you must realize that not every action will be perfect. Not every action will produce the desired result. Not every action will work. Making mistakes, getting it almost right, and experimenting to see what happens are all part of the process of eventually getting it right."

# I Believe I Can Fly

The title of a song that was extremely popular in 1996. Originally written as part of the soundtrack for the movie "Space Jam," it actually has become the most popular song for its writer and initial performer – R. Kelly. Space Jam is an interesting movie (one that I have not seen) that features Looney Tunes characters and Michael Jordan. An additional bit of trivia is that R. Kelly actually played semi-professional basketball.

In general, this song is about learning to reach the stars (reach your dreams) and about believing that you can become something great. It is saying believe you can go far in life and get to where you want to get to. For some, this was a new message, and for others, it is a reminder.

This should not just be a popular song. It should be a daily affirmation. Every day, I have to believe that I can fly, even if I do not feel like it. Every day, I have to believe I can go far in life, even while I am yet taking baby steps. I have to believe that I can (and will) get where I want to go. I believe I will get to the place the Father has prepared for me, doing those things He has created me to do.

Personally, it is ironic that this message refers to flying. I do not like flying. Yes, I am a Gold Medallion Delta Sky-miler which suggests I do a lot of flying, but that still does not mean I have to enjoy the experience. I fly, confident that the airplane will take me where I am trying to go. Life is the same, I have to believe that the steps I am taking, while sometimes scary, sometimes frightening, like turbulence on the planes, I will get to where I want to go.

I believe I can fly. I have no choice. I have to.

# Rubber Bands

What do people use to hold things together these days? None of the school supply lists have rubber bands on them. In fact, rubber bands are even hard to find these days, which raises my question of what people use these days to hold things together.

Binder clips? Twist ties? There are lots of things that can do the work of a rubber band. How do I know? It only took a look in my office desk drawer to see the myriad of things that seem to have replaced the well-known rubber band. (No, I did not find any rubber bands in my stash.) This made me wonder what it was we had to hold together in the old days that even required rubber bands… all I could think of were pens and pencils. Maybe index cards that we were using to develop our papers for school. Wow. Things sure have changed. There are pencil cases of all kinds to store pens and pencils, and I personally do not know anyone still using index cards to take notes for their research. But have things really changed that much?

In life, we still need things that hold us together. We need things that are flexible and resilient. We need things that support us as we go from day to day… simple things, like binder clips or rubber bands. For me, the things that are the binder clips in my life are my family and friends. Friends hold me together when I sometimes cannot hold myself together. Friends remind me what I am made of and capable of. They remind me who I am. My rubber bands are my faith and the memories of the many times that God has carried me over and through, nudging flexibility from me in situations that required me to hold it together. These situations required me to stretch and not break, and to stretch yet not give out. Sometimes I have had to be stretched beyond my natural limits, that is, beyond what I thought I could bear. And yet, after going through, I am "back in shape," back to where I was, just like the rubber band that returns to its shape after it has been stretched.

What is your rubber band? It is not for me to know, just to encourage you to have one so when the time comes, you will be confident of what holds you together.

# Golf Lessons

In Florida, there is a golf course about every 1000 feet… or so it seems. Gorgeous green landscapes with flourishing florals and fascinating fauna (I have always wanted to use that word). It adds a great option to going to the beach and it is pandemic approved.

For the record, I am not a golfer. I play at golf. Yes, I have a set of clubs—ladies' clubs–designed for my height, and I have the shoes and the outfits. I also have the ladies' balls and the gloves, and I am qualified to drive the cart. Aren't those the essentials?

With all the courses available, I figured it was time for some lessons. Then I could take advantage of the beautiful courses available to me.

First lesson: All the lessons do not take place on the course. It has been said that Tiger Woods plays every golf course in his head, all 18 holes, before he ever sets foot on the course. Besides making me tired before I ever got started, I realized that there are things that separate the novice from the elite. At the elite level, what separates good athletes from great athletes is often related to their mindset. "As a man thinketh, so is he," Proverbs 23:7 (KJV), can even loosely be applied to golf.  The life lesson in this is that we need to think through where we are trying to go before we get there. This cannot be done without trusting God, and then understanding what we are signing up for before we get on the course. Think things through.

Second lesson: Keep your eye on the ball. This is a phrase used in every sport… think about soccer. There is no point in even being on the field and in the game if you are not watching the ball. I learned this is even more important in golf, since the ball is so small. (Can you say visually challenged?) Thank goodness they make pink balls for ladies. In golf, it is not just looking at the ball that is important; you also have to focus on the part of the ball you need to hit, based on what you are trying to do. You hit it in one place to tee off, and a different place to putt. Proverbs 4:25 (NIV) encourages us: "Let your eyes look directly ahead and let your gaze be fixed straight in front of you." The model prayer, found in Matthew 6:11, teaches us "give us this day." Life lesson: Focus on what is in front of you, keeping in mind that it is not what is in front of you that determines the outcome, it is how you handle it. It is how you hit the ball.

Third lesson: the real test is not in keeping the ball out of the rough but in getting out after you hit one in the rough. On a golf course, the rough is that long (taller) grass around the fairway and the green. It is the place where your ball hides in plain sight. It is that place that eats balls almost better than the water. For people like me, telling me to avoid the rough is like telling me to hit in the rough. Life lesson: it is the same when we know not to do something, and we do it anyway! We know the life situations we need to avoid, the people and things we need to stay away from, yet we seem to be drawn to them. That is our rough in life. And yes, it is a lot tougher to get out of these life situations that we create than it was to get in them. Avoid the rough. We have guidance and instruction from the best teacher there is on the course called life: "Now flee from youthful lusts and pursue righteousness, faith, love and peace, with those who call on the Lord from a pure heart," 2 Timothy 2:22 NASB.

While on the course and really struggling to put all the lessons together, I also practiced the art of letting others "play through." Sometimes when you are on the course and things just aren't working out like you need, and you can't quite get it together—you step aside and let the other golfers on the course play through. As I spent quite a bit of time looking for balls in the rough, I learned to let others play through.

Bonus lesson: play at your own speed and do not let others rush you.

# *Bunch of Grapes*

Words are interesting. There are a lot of different words that are used to define more than one of something. Generally, these are called collective nouns. According to grammar-monster.com "A collective noun is the word used to represent a group of people, animals, or things." We all know from elementary school English class that a noun by itself is a person, place, or thing. Put these two together and you have a way to describe a group of people (a team), a group of animals (a school of fish), or things (a fleet of ships). But this is not really the way we talk. When there is more than one of something, we are more apt to say "it's a bunch." There were a bunch of fish in the water or a bunch of ships at the pier. Just like "Mom went to the grocery and bought a bunch of grapes." A bunch of grapes, a bunch of bananas–we are used to things coming in bunches.

But, there are other things that we do not want in bunches, or that we do not want multiples of: things like challenges and adversity. One challenge at a time is about all most of us can handle, or maybe two. A bunch of challenges? Whether we like it or not, our days come with bunches of challenges. Traffic, rain with no umbrella, a hot water heater that is only producing cold water, a low tire symbol on the new car... we would prefer that these "opportunities" come one at a time, but like most things–they come in bunches. What is the collective noun for these bunches of things? It is called life.

Life is a series, a collection, a group, a cluster, a clover (use whichever one gives you a sense of relief)... there is a relatively lighthearted saying (or superstition, you decide) "if it's not one thing, it's another." My family has modified this over the years to be "if it's not one thing, it's another... on page 1." It's our way of saying there are usually pages of things, not just one or two things.

Bunches. If things in life work in our favor, we get our life bunches one item at a time. It is kind of like eating grapes or bananas. They may come in bunches, clusters, or a handful, but you eat them one at a time. Whether they are served up one at a time or in groups–the real opportunity is in how we deal with them. One at a time. Like small grapes, sometimes you can do two at a time, but mostly focusing on one at the time. I recall teaching my granddaughter to eat grapes. We started with cutting them into quarters, then progressed to halves and then, when I was sure she could (and would) chew before swallowing, we went to whole grapes. With the whole grapes came the ability to have several in front of her. She had matured to know that while there where several in front of her, they could only be safely eaten one at a time.

Life serves us bunches of challenges and opportunities. When it does, and it will, let's treat them like bunches of grapes. Tackle them one at a time.

"My brethren, count it all joy when you fall into various trials, knowing that the testing of your faith produces patience. But let patience have *its* perfect work, that you may be perfect and complete, lacking nothing," James 1:2-4 (NKJV).

# When and If

I do words for a living. Words, the order in which we use them, and the punctuation we use with them, convey so much. A lot of what is being conveyed gets missed, because we do not stop to apply the real meanings of the words. Two of the most often missed are when and if.

Imagine these sentences… "When you have time, will you get me some water," or, "If you have time, will you get me some water?"

Now insert the real meaning of these words: "at or on which" you have time, will you get me some water, or "in case" you have time, will you get me some water…

Let's make it simple. One says at the point where you have a break, will you get me some water. The other says, if there is a possibility that arises where you can, will you get me some water. One is a certainty; the other is a possibility.

These same conditions apply to life. There are some things that are a certainty; some say death and taxes. There are other things that are just a possibility, like winning the lottery.

# For That Reason...

Therefore. It is an adverb that loosely means... for that reason. I do words for a living and generally when you write "therefore", it means that some idea or thought has been presented before the use of the word. (More than you want to know, but may come in handy during your stint as a homeschool teacher.)

I have a new normal and it is wreaking havoc on my weekly planning time.

I cannot visit my favorite restaurant; therefore, I am going to simply go to the freezer, open the door and stand there like a teenager, and produce an idea for dinner. I cannot plan window shopping at the bookstore; therefore, I will look on my shelves of books and find something to read. I cannot go see my baby sister for her birthday, therefore I will make sure everyone has the invitation to the virtual birthday party. I cannot start my plan to go to see my mother for a visit, therefore I will spend some time today gathering all the pictures I have of her and use them to warm my heart.

I cannot do so many things that were part of my life before this "new normal", therefore I will stop dwelling on what I can't do and focus on being grateful for what I can do. For that reason (therefore), I am putting the top down and going riding on the freeway.

# Confessions of a Workaholic

I am a workaholic.

There, I said it. For all those people, (I love y'all) that say this to my face on a regular basis, I am finally agreeing with you. Yes, I am a workaholic. But – for those same people... I do want to provide a definition and some context.

The definition is "a person who works compulsively." But keep reading... it also says, "the term generally implies that the person enjoys their work, but it can also alternately imply that they simply feel compelled to do it," (Peters, 2017).[19]

I am a workaholic. Every day, I work to strengthen my relationship with the Lord. Every day, I am compelled to thank Him for his goodness and favor towards me.

I am a workaholic. Every day I work to be a better person. I am compelled to try. One of my daily affirmations is, "Every day, in every way, I am getting better."

I am a workaholic. Every day, I work to get my heart rate up for at least 30 minutes. I am compelled to be healthier.

I am a workaholic. Every day, I work to find at least 5 things to be grateful for... and I write them down in case I get forgetful.

I am a workaholic. Every day, I work to find at least 10 people I can pray for and diligently throughout the day pray specifically for them. (You can do this by praying for someone at the top of each hour.)

I am a workaholic. Every day, I work to let the people I love know that I love them and to try and make sure they experience my love for them.

Yes, I am a workaholic. I work my mind, my body, and my spirit. I enjoy this journey of becoming a better person, every day, in every way.

In the words of Rick Ross and Vivica Fox... every day, I'm Hustlin'.

# Side Effects

I am currently taking more medications than I would like. The last couple of weeks have reminded me of the several minutes of disclaimers that every commercial for a medication includes. It is a bit daunting when what is supposed to help you has an equal, if not greater, chance of harming you. The more time I spend researching the side effects of all the medications the doctors are proposing, the more I realize that almost everything in life has side effects.

For example. Eating healthy is supposed to help our overall health. Fresh vegetables, fruits, organic. Side effect... this will cause serious harm to your budget and your bank account.

Sheltering in place has also had some interesting side effects. Staying at home helped prevent the spread of the coronavirus. Staying at home also reduced expenses for gas and some of the other costs associated with going to work in an office every day. Side effects: Many gained COVID pounds that seem to appear overnight from all the snacking that takes place. Side effects: many are getting to know, I mean really know, the people that live in the house with them... and not everyone likes each other. Sheltering in place kept us safe from the pandemic but left side effects, many of which have not yet come to light.

I do not want you to think that all side effects are bad. Some medications cause weight loss (trust me, I am not taking any of those) and that could be a good thing. Others cause you to be sleepy, and for some of my Type A friends, that is the only way to get them to slow down.

What is the real message? Everything in life has side effects. With that wonderful new husband comes in-laws... side effects. With that beautiful new baby comes 2AM feedings… side effects. Our job is to do the research... ahead of time... not to avoid the side effects, but to know what we are signing up for and to ask God to prepare us for what is ahead.

"Surely there comes a time when counting the cost and paying the price are not things to think about any more. All that matters is value - the ultimate value of what one does." ~ James Hilton, English novelist.

# Homeschooling

I do words for a living. Homeschooling... Phyllis Lee was my English teacher. She was also perhaps the sweetest mean person I ever met. Sorry, words matter. I should say she was the most rigid and disciplined person I ever met. If you do not know how to diagram a sentence... well?

God reminded me this morning that just like I diagram sentences EVERY day I need to diagram this situation with the same approach. Believe me, I never imagined sentence structure would be a useful skill while enduring Mrs. Lee's class. If you are ~60 then you likely heard... "How things are done the adverbs tell - as quickly, slowly, badly or well."

So, today, take time to diagram your situation. Diagram your situation. Find your noun, find your verb, but do not forget the adverb. What needs to be done, quickly, slowly and hopefully, always well.

Ephesians 3:20 (ESV), "Now to Him who is able to do exceedingly abundantly above all that we ask or think, according to the power that works in us."

I will let you figure out the noun and the verb (nouns and active verbs were not part of today's lesson, that's homework) but make sure you spend some time on the adverb. Thank you, Phyllis Lee.

# Walking Is Faster

Walking is faster than running. I started running again. It is the easiest way for me to get my heart rate up, it helps me lose weight and I can do it without thinking... or so I thought. After several knee surgeries, several foot surgeries, an impending hip surgery, and enough pins and screws in my body to set off a metal detector, it was clearly an admirable goal.

Shoes check, ear buds check, hit the pavement. Somewhere in this process I failed to let my body know what was about to take place. Prior to this "I'll just run" idea, I was walking every day. Two miles a day, a slow leisurely pace. Slow is the key word. I somehow thought running would be faster than walking. It is not. Or at least not in the ways that matter.

After that first run (it is supposed to come back to you, just like riding a bike) ... I realized just how out of shape I was. All I could do was think about the last time I told people that I loved them because it felt like I was surely going to die. Every step and every breath. Important part of running, once you run out, you have to run (or hobble) back in. My heart rate was definitely up, I surely was losing weight (I was sweating like a racehorse), but I was having to do a lot of thinking. You know, I think I can, I think I can. I think I know where the nearest hospital is, I think the insurance card is in my wallet and easy to access, I think I will scar up my face when I fall flat ... thinking.

Compare that to walking. I am able to be kind to my body... my knees and feet do not swell. I am able to have the confidence that I will be able to return from my walk without assistance. And it is faster. Faster to get me to a place of peace. Faster to get me to notice my surroundings. Faster to get me to stop and speak to my neighbors. Faster to get me to look up at the sky. Faster to get me to remembering the awesomeness of God. Faster to get to a place of peace.

To Alison, the running coach, I bested my pace today. I got to my place of peace within minutes and even had time to snap a few photos.

Philippians 4:7 (NIV), "And the peace of God which transcends all understanding, will guard your hearts and minds in Christ."

# Reasons

Everything happens for a reason. Good stuff, and yes, bad stuff, happens for a reason. Is the reason important?

I am beginning to understand that "why" it happened is not as important as "what" I am supposed to do after it happens.

Life really is like a roller coaster, up, down, twists and turns and anyone who knows me, really knows me, knows I do not like roller coasters. God, with his sense of humor has put so many ups and downs and twists and turns in my life that there is no need for roller coaster rides – just keep living.

There sure have been an abundance of ups and downs, twists and turns in my life recently. Again, it is not the why, but the what. When you ride a roller coaster, you strap in, find a place to get a good grip, hold your breath, say some prayers ... and then it takes off. While riding you scream sometimes, tell yourself you are never going to do it again, say some bad things about the people who should have stopped you from getting on it the first place, say some other bad things about the people who are riding with you and seem to be enjoying the ride... and then it ends. You catch your breath, fix your wig, put a smile on your face, and a strut in your walk... and come off the ride like it was the best thing you have ever done.

That's the what! After you go through, remember that you GOT through.... and you do not have to look like what you went through.

# Temporary Pause

This is where most books have a conclusion or an ending. I am choosing to call this a temporary pause. There is more to come.

Every day, I wake up thankful and grateful that God has allowed me another day, another chance. Thankful and grateful, but no longer scared. Thankful that He sees fit to look beyond all that I have done to disappoint Him. Grateful that He has enough confidence in me to give me another chance. But I am no longer scared of what the day is going to offer. I am not afraid of whether I can handle whatever is ahead.

I still spend my mornings in conversation with God, asking, and more often than not - pleading, for Him to show me what to do, how to do, and when to do. .

My Morning Musings. My guiding genius. Words that often come faster than I can comprehend and always faster than I can write. I no longer seek to understand what I am supposed to do with what I am being given.

Since I do words for a living, I write.

I am still musing in the mornings, and I pray God will continue to have confidence in me to share them with others.

Live well and be blessed.

# Bibliography

1. Merriam-Webster. (n.d.). Muse. In Merriam-Webster.com dictionary. Retrieved from https://www.merriam-webster.com/dictionary/muse

2. Yahoo.com (n.d.). New. In Yahoo.com dictionary. Retrieved from (https://search.yahoo.com/search?fr=mcafee&type=E211US105G0&p=definition+of+new)

3. Yahoo.com (n.d.). Anew. In Yahoo.com dictionary. Retrieved from https://search.yahoo.com/search;_ylt=Awr FE2tZHbNkPtEfV65XNyoA;_ylc=X1MDMjc2NjY3OQ RfcgMyBGZyA21jYWZlZQRmcjIDc2ItdG9wBGdwcmlk A2lkclpWZ09UUXJPeXBWVnRoc291MkEEbl9yc2x0Az AEbl9zdWdnAzEwBG9yaWdpbgNzZWFyY2gueWFob28u Y29tBHBvcwMwBHBxc3RyAwRwcXN0cmwDMARxc3 RybAMxOARxdWVyeQNkZWZpbml0aW9uJTIwb2Yl MjBhbmV3BHRfc3RtcAMxNjg5NDYwMjI?p=definition+of+anew&fr2=sb-top&fr=mcafee&type=E211US105G0

4. Department of Veteran's Affairs. (n.d.). *America's wars.* Retrieved from https://www.va.gov/opa/publications/factsheets/fs_americas_wars.pdf#:~:text=America%E2%80%99s%20Wars%20Total%20%281775%20-1991%29%20U.S.%20Military%20Service,Living%20Veterans%20%28Periods%20of%20War%20%26%20Peace%29%2019%2C210%2C000

5. Minneapolismn.gov (n.d.). *Police department.*
Retrieved from https://www.minneapolismn.gov/
government/departments/police/

6. TheNewRevivalProject. (n.d.). *Toby Mac – City
on our knees (official music video)* [Video]. YouTube.
https://www.youtube.com/watch?v=yWcR84DOr5c

7. Dictionary.com (n.d.). Dwell. In Dictionary.com.
Retrieved from https://www.dictionary.com/browse/dwell

8. Bible Study Tools (n.d.). *What does the bible say about
restoration?* Retrieved from https://www.biblestudytools.com
/search/?q=rest&t=niv&c=all

9. National Hurricane Center (n.d.). *Tropical cyclone
climatology.*
Retrieved from https://www.nhc.noaa.gov/climo/

10. Scott, A. (2023, June 9). *The forgotten history of father's
day.* Retrieved from https://www.almanac.com/forgotten-
history-fathers-day

11. Wikipedia (n.d.). *Baseball.* Retrieved from https://
en.wikipedia.org/wiki/Baseball

12. Wikipedia (n.d.). Paradox. Retrieved from https://
en.wikipedia.org/wiki/Paradox

13. Dictionary.com (n.d.). Grind. In Dictionary.com
Retrieved from https://www.dictionary.com/browse/grind

14. Simmons, G. (n.d.). *Me, Inc. Build an army of one...*
Retrieved from https://www.goodreads.com/en/book/
show/23437552

15. Dictionary.com (n.d.). Valley. In Dictionary.com Retrieved from https://www.dictionary.com/browse/valley

16. Wikipedia (n.d.). Decision Tree. Retrieved from https://en.wikipedia.org/wiki/Decision_tree

17. Wikipedia (n.d.). Goal. Retrieved from https://en.wikipedia.org/wiki/Goal

18. Goolsby Jr., J. (2018, January 10). *Faithful over a few things*. Retrieved from *https://www.macon.com/living/religion/article193896209.html#:~:text=Matthew%20 25%3A23%3A%20His%20lord,the%20joy%20of%20 your%20lord.%E2%80%9D*

19. Peters, B. (4 Oct. 2017). *Workaholism vs. passion vs. boredom.* Retrieved from: https://medium.com/@Brian_G_ Peters/workaholism-vs-passion-vs-boredom-how-to-get-ahead-without-burning-out-ed50ffecfe41